IP: DIY

INTERNET PORNOGRAPHY:

DO-IT-YOURSELF TREATMENT GUIDE FOR MEN

Dr Phil Watts

Ogilvie Publishing
Perth, Western Australia

Copyright

This book is copyrighted. Apart from that permitted under the Copyright Act 1968 (Cwlth), no portion can be reproduced or copied in any form, or by any means, without prior written permission from the author.

© P. Watts

IP: DIY - Internet Pornography: Do-It-Yourself Treatment Guide for Men / Author: Watts, Phil, 1962

1st Edition

Ogilvie Publishing
PO Box 393
South Perth, 6951
Western Australia

ISBN: 978-0-975604-23-6 (paperback)
ISBN: 978-0-975604-24-3 (ebook)

Subjects: Internet pornography.
            Computer sex.
            Pornography.
            Sex addiction--Treatment.
            Internet addiction--Treatment.
            Sex addicts--Rehabilitation.

Dewey Number: 616.85833

Editing and indexing by Linda McNamara

Typesetting by Regan Timu

Orders www.drphil.com.au

Dedication

This book is dedicated to those men who want to free themselves from the entrapment of pornography issues. I also dedicate it to the boys of the future who will have to deal with these issues in the years to come. In doing so, I add a prayer that my son Jarom will not become one of those men who need this book

Acknowledgements

As I put the final touches to my fourth book, I would like to express my gratitude to the profession of psychology. It has allowed me to help so many people across a diverse range of subjects. I consider it an honour and privilege to have been able to contribute to the understanding of these topics and, in particular, to assist with educating others about (and thereby aiding the treatment for) problems associated with pornography.

I acknowledge those clever pioneering professionals from whom I have learnt, and whose ideas I have adapted and modified in this book, to assist the lives of men in dire need. Some of the sources are listed at the end of the book, and I thank each of those professionals for their contributions. I hope that they see my work as an expansion of their ideas, however, I apologise if I have not given a complete reference to their work.

Two colleagues have been particularly helpful. Simon Kennedy, a clinical and forensic psychologist in Melbourne who is also trained in sex therapy, provided reassurance that the book covered the major topics. Peter Howell of LDS social services assisted by providing some helpful exercises and ensuring the book's suitability for religious readers. I am deeply appreciative to them for their perspectives and assistance.

I am grateful to the men who have sought treatment. Through their journeys I have been able to refine the techniques incorporated in this book. I have shared some of their stories – some in frank detail (with the permission of a brave few who said I could), or with details disguised to simply provide their healing stories.

I am deeply appreciative of my trusty team who help to turn Phil's ramblings into a coherent and readable book. I sincerely thank my editor and indexer, Linda McNamara, who has an expert eye for detail and a brilliant command of language. I also acknowledge Regan Timu, who painstakingly typeset the layout of the book, and Peter at Artproof printing for producing the copies.

No book can be written without the help of family. I am eternally indebted to my loving wife Bethwyn for her support and encouragement in all aspects of my life, including my writing. I also have to acknowledge my delightful children, Jarom and Arielle, who inspire me to make the world a better place.

Contents

Acknowledgements iv

Preface ix

Introduction 1

Chapter 1 – Setting the Scene

    The Self-help Journey 10

    Your Best Friend 16

Chapter 2 – The Problems

    The Internet Addiction Test 23

    What's My Problem? 27

    Compulsive Nature 31

    Damaging Relationships 37

    Moral Integrity 41

    Illegal and Dangerous Acts 45

Chapter 3 – Facts and Information
>   Some Facts about Pornography 49
>   What is Common? 59
>   What is Pornography? 66

Chapter 4 – The Brain and Other Factors
>   The Brain Pathways 73
>   Two Sides to Every Brain 86
>   Chemical Cocktails, Sexual Release, and Depression .. 91

Chapter 5 – What Causes the Problem?
>   Tunnel and the Funnel 100
>   Why That Image? 107
>   Timeline and Patterns 113
>   The Two-part Problem 123
>   Keeping Safe 127
>   Looking at Illegal Material 132

Chapter 6 – Cognitive and Behavioural Therapy
>   Functional Behavioural Assessment 138
>   A (Antecedents) – Triggers 143
>   Internal Triggers 151

Thoughts 158
Behaviour 168
Practical Strategies 174
Time Management 180
Consequences 186

Chapter 7 – Important Treatment Strategies
Paradoxical Keys to Change 190
Sexuality 203
The Golden Key to Success 216

Chapter 8 – Other Important Points
Spirituality 223
Partners and Their Reactions 232
Protecting Society 242
Concluding Remarks 246

Useful Resources 248

Index 250

Table of Exercises 255

About the Author 256

Preface

I have watched with awe the rapid advances of new technology over the last 30 years. Things I never thought possible have suddenly become the norm. Simple things such as sending a picture or letter via email were not thought possible when I started university. The new technology helps make day-to-day existence easier in so many ways, and the benefits to society from the rapidly changing computer applications have been huge. Sadly, I have also dealt with the causalities of this revolution as an ever-increasing number of people are drawn into compulsive behaviours made possible by this new technology. Their lives spiral out of control through the different experiences made possible by the Internet.

I am fascinated with how quickly each new technological advance also brings forth alternative ways for the delivery of both pornographic material and other behavioural interests through computer applications. I would love to be able to study all of the different phenomena and write a series of books about online gaming, virtual life addictions, cyber-infidelity through chat, and the many other patterns of excessive behaviour which, in their extremes, are destroying people's lives. While the reasons people engage in these behaviours overlap, problems related to Internet pornography is the area of most concern to me.

I watch an ever-increasing number of men coming into my clinical practice, or the practices of my colleagues, with completely out of control behaviours. Their lives are impacted because they jeopardise their intimate relationships, suffer legal problems, or experience moral and spiritual destruction. My concern is that it is not just men with a history of major dysfunction, but people from relatively normal lives and backgrounds who are becoming drawn into patterns of behaviour which are destroying their lives.

This book needed to be written. Originally I began to write a book on this topic designed for therapists, but I subsequently had to stop and refocus on the treatment needs of men. Perhaps the book designed for educating therapists will be finished one day, but at this point in time I have to share some of my methods for helping those men whose lives are currently out of control. While I will continue to educate therapists through my training courses, my current priority is to provide something to make a practical difference in the community. In effect, I want this book to be a tool box to provide immediate help to those who need it.

I am writing this book for men – not because I am sexist, or think that women do not have a pornography problem or problems with Internet compulsions – but because I believe there is a particular psychology, coupled with a unique attraction to visual images, which reacts upon men's brains to cause a set of problems which are stronger and far more prevalent for men than for women. There are many more men in need of help at this moment in time.

If you have picked up this book, you are probably one of three different types of reader. You may be someone whose life is out of control and therefore battling with feelings of powerlessness as you go back again and again to look at images; you may be a man's spouse or family member, trying to make sense of the changes in his behaviour and, in particular, the reasons why he cannot or will not stop; or you may be a professional looking for some guidance in managing a client's behaviour. All of you will find some useful ideas in this book. First and foremost, however, this is a practical treatment guide.

The psychological research into treatment technologies is far behind the rapid advances in technology. This book is not a complete answer, and 10 or 15 years from now it may be obsolete, but I have attempted to find the best strategies available at this point in time. As this is not a textbook I have kept references to a minimum, however, I have provided a list of useful resources to indicate where the ideas in this book have been derived. I am grateful for the wonderful ideas being developed by others and I am therefore not presenting the material in this book as purely my own work. Many ideas have been borrowed and adapted from others. I trust you will find some pearls of wisdom to assist you in your quest for a better life.

Dr Phil Watts

Introduction

Thank you for having the courage to open this book. It takes guts to face a problem and, as the title indicates, this book is for men experiencing problems with Internet pornography. That does not mean that women seeking to understand their partner's behaviour, or people without problems, cannot look at the book. However, this book is not written for those people. It is for you, a man with a problem. In writing this for you, I have made some assumptions about you and your journey, based on my experience in treating Internet compulsions.

My first assumption is that you must be a man of courage to begin to face your problem, seek answers, and want to change. This courage is essential. In psychology we know that those who face a fear will get better and those who avoid the fear will stay the same or get worse. It is the same with this particular problem – if you face the fact that you have a problem, you can get better.

My second assumption is that you are not a dirty pervert or a sick and twisted individual, a point to which I will refer repeatedly in this book. You are an individual who could come from any walk of life, be it bus driver, accountant, computer programmer or labourer. Research suggests that you are probably better educated than the average person and aged from 16 to 95 years old. Why do I assume that? Because I have seen others like you, from all walks of life and leading seemingly normal lives, but who are out of control on the Internet.

Some of you will have other problems. Depression and anxiety are very common conditions amongst Internet pornography users. The book contains specific sections and exercises to help you work out what may be triggering the behaviour. You will then be able to address those triggers to help you to reduce your need to look at Internet pornography.

The types of pornographic images looked at on the Internet can vary widely. Some people, but not all, look at illegal images. You may be one of those who only look at soft-core images, which are legally available, or you may be attracted to images that other members of society could find repugnant, revolting, degrading or demeaning. If you are in the latter category, you may need some extra help with treatment.

As your use of the Internet took hold, you lost some of yourself. I would like remind you, even before we begin to discuss the issue, that there is more to you than just this problem. I see you as a good man doing things that may be bad for you and for those around you. You are more than the images you look at. The shame associated with this behaviour, and the double life you are leading to hide this problem, will have taken a toll upon you. Together, we need to help you rediscover who you are and help you regain your self-worth.

My third assumption is that the power to change is within you. You are reading this book because the Internet is controlling you and you feel that you have lost your power to choose. The factor that separates someone who is functional from someone with a problem is the ability to choose and then act upon those choices. I believe that you have many of the resources, capacities and capabilities which, with a little guidance, can be very effective in changing this behaviour.

I make no apologies in saying that what you are dealing with is an extremely hard problem to beat. If it was easy you would not need to read self-help books or visit a therapist. If it was easy I would not see men in therapy. It is a hard path back to self-control.

In psychology there is a debate as to whether to call the excessive use of pornography an addiction or a compulsion and whether it is a new condition or just a variation of things we have had forever. From a professional point of view there are differences between addictions and compulsions, but for you it really does not matter what we call it, it is the beast you need to fight. I have chosen to call it a "pornography problem" because problems can be solved and fixed. Books like *Men Are From Mars, Women Are From Venus* tell us that men are good problem-solvers. Addiction makes you feel as if you have a defect which will prevent you from beating that addiction. A compulsion is an irresistible urge which is difficult to overcome and makes you feel powerless.

I do not doubt that some of these factors are involved, but throughout this book I use the term "pornography problem" as a reminder to you that you are going to use your abilities to help address this situation. The power is within you.

My fourth assumption is that you will have relapses. Why do I say that you are going to relapse before you even start? I don't want you to lose heart and become despondent when the going gets tough, because I have never seen anybody give up something that is hard to give up without a fight. Everybody has a unique journey, but what is not unique is that people pick up a book or go to therapy during a low point in a crisis (for example, getting caught out by a partner, getting in trouble at work, or experiencing legal problems).. The crisis triggers the need to seek help.

Once you seek help and begin to get an answer there is a degree of excitement, a return of hope, and an increasing sense of control as something that has been a problem for a very long time is gradually overcome. Early feelings of being in control of the behaviour, rather than the behaviour controlling you, can be ecstatic moments in a depressing existence. There is a good feeling and motivation is high.

Then along comes a slip-up. It may occur after days or months, but in acute stress (a careless moment or an exciting trigger) a little part of your brain begins to itch, nag and torment. At first you push the thoughts away, but they keep coming back. Due to the excuses you make, you switch off the conscious part of your brain control and allow yourself to indulge in the behaviour. As the behaviour finishes, a second stage kicks in.

This second stage in some ways is where you feel even worse than you did before you started treatment. I remember that for years my father smoked cigarettes and he always said *"I could give up if I wanted to, I just don't want to"*. It is an easy justification because when you try to give up and find that you are unable, you realise that the problem is bigger than you thought it was. That makes you feel smaller and more powerless than you ever felt before. It is even harder if you relapse after having had professional help, or have made a serious effort to control the problem. The question plaguing you will be: *"Is there any chance I can get better?"*

As a psychologist who, for over 20 years, has worked with different problematic behaviour (including addictions to alcohol and drugs, eating disorders, gambling, compulsive spending and stealing), I have formed the view that Internet pornography is equal to, or harder than, any of these conditions to overcome, particularly for people who are seriously out of control.

If willpower alone was enough to give up, you would have given up before now. You may have previously made a tremendous effort to will the problem away. My argument is that willpower is not sufficient to bring about the change. Picture a tug of war situation. You stand at one end of the rope, the Internet pornography problem is at the other end, and there is a large and scary pit between the two. Through sheer willpower you will try hard to pull the rope in opposition to the problem, trying to pull it into the pit. The more you pull, the more the problem pulls back. That is simple psychology. The solution is not to pull more – it is to let go of the rope. If you let go of the rope you will have to find something else to do. Letting go of the rope is not easy.

If your car breaks down at the side of the road you can will the car to move all you like, but it will not move unless somebody fixes the engine. You need to develop strategies to get the car moving, rather than just sitting in the car trying to will it to move. But don't despair – your willpower is needed. I want you to apply the force of your will and determination to the tools provided in this book.

Research on willpower indicates that we have a finite amount of willpower and, therefore, the greater the number of decisions you make, the less willpower you have leftover. One of the goals of this book is to help you to allocate your resources to enable you to function effectively. You will need to find a way to increase your willpower store as you let the rope go.

A phoenix rises out of the ashes. In my opinion, the real work of recovery can only take place after you reach the lowest point. It is when you reach the lowest point that you truly understand and admit where the problem lies. It is at this point that you begin the real work. You are then in a position to regain your control and to reclaim your life.

I can promise you that it will be an interesting journey which at times may cause you to lose hope. However, I would ask that from time to time you review the Key Points in this section to remind yourself of the journey. It is important that you always remember the underlying assumptions I have made about you and your journey of recovery.

Key Points

Assumption

- You are a man with the courage to face your demons. It takes considerable courage to stop something in your life which is powerful.

- You are a good man doing things that might be bad for you. Some behaviour is bad, but people are good. Never forget that.

- The power to change is within you. No-one but you can change you.

- There will be relapses on the road to recovery. Do not use this as an excuse for self-indulgence, but learn from every action both good and bad.

Exercise 1 – Assumptions Reminder Card

In your own words, list the assumptions on a card or poster to act as a reminder. Place it somewhere handy for a quick review. On a regular basis, review the assumptions I have made about you and your journey. The purpose of this is to activate the parts of the brain that can see your positive aspects. You may find that repeating the assumptions regularly, like an affirmation, can help them to become an automatic thought pattern.

Exercise 2 – Reflections Journal

Buy yourself a book, or set up a secure space on your computer, to be your self-treatment journal. This is a space to allow you to reflect upon the material in this book and to draw connections with your life. This needs to be a private place for you to express your feelings. One client described is as place to "vomit up" his feelings. Put like that it sounds a bit disgusting, but you need to capture and express your thoughts and ideas as they emerge.

People do not get better simply by reading a book such as this one. This is a book to work through. As you read about the material that is relevant to you, take the time to enter comments and reactions in your journal.

In key sections in this book, I will also remind you to reflect and enter comments into your journal about certain key concepts.

1
Setting the Scene

The Self-help Journey

This book aims to educate and then to encourage you to practice the skills you've learned. The next few sections are very important for helping you to identify if you have a problem and, if so, which aspects of the problem are affecting you. There are some worksheets and exercises for you to complete. Other than some questionnaires printed in this book, you will need to draw up the worksheets described in the exercises. This has been done to keep the book small and portable. Please make and use the worksheets to analyse where the problem is coming from because, unless you do something to change the emotional reactions, the outcome will not change. Intellectual understanding does not resolve these problems.

The answers you give to the worksheets are designed to help determine which aspects are going to be the focus of your individual treatment. Later in the book you will find some sections which are relevant to your problem and others which are not. For example, there are some men who come to my practice who are highly religious and engaged in behaviours contrary to the beliefs of their faith. Shame and guilt are extremely high because the behaviour is completely inconsistent with other areas of their life. They are internally tormented. There are other men who have no guilt about the behaviour because pornography is just a part of life, but their partner is complaining about changes within the intimacy of their relationship, and the lack of sexual contact and affection. This is an example of external pressure. More extreme external pressures on some men are legal problems arising out of their behaviour. Therefore, to gain control, there are common elements for all three of these different types of Internet pornography users, but there are also specific elements for each type of user. It makes sense that even though everybody is different, there are common patterns to their problems.

Following the opportunity to self-assess, I will provide you with some facts to help you understand your problem behaviour. This will include some general facts about the prevalence and the nature of Internet compulsions. Because men like facts and need to understand what causes a problem, I want you to be informed as much possible about the Internet pornography problem. Taking the time to understand where the problem is coming from, and how common the problem is, adds a level of reassurance and begins to be a platform for rebuilding self-confidence. However, the practical reality for most people is that facts alone are not going to fix the problem.

The balance of the book is then divided into two parts. The first part is designed to explain the dynamics of the compulsive behaviour and to try and give you some simple models to explain what is happening to you. I will then look at strategies to help you gain control. You have a responsibility to yourself to practice the exercises as much as possible.

There are arguments about whether to address the underlying cause. When people come to my office they say *"Dr Phil, can you cure me?"* My first response to that question is to say that I can give you strategies to help, which most people find are highly beneficial for gaining control and managing the behaviour. As you hear about *"control"* and *"manage"*, there is a part of you which will say *"I don't want to spend the rest of my life managing, I want the problem to go away"*. Well, the bad news for you is that looking at pornography excessively over a long period of time has brought about an alteration to your brain. As much as possible, I will help you to learn strategies to rewire your brain and your thinking, and to develop a healthy life. Ultimately, this is a big challenge. Some of my clients achieve it. Other people will spend the rest of their life managing the problem.

In general, those who successfully resolve the issue have had to completely review their life. This includes changing how they deal with situations emotionally, addressing their sexuality and repairing relationships, changing the way they deal with stress and anxiety, and redesigning their thoughts and beliefs; in fact it is a total psychological makeover.

Before you put the book down and look for an alternative five minute cure, all I can say is that you need to do this. You need to do it for those around you, such as your spouse or partner, your children, your God, or for whatever else matters to you. Ultimately, you have to do it for you. Our lives are too short to allow ourselves to be consumed by our problems. I once read a bumper sticker that said *"Life is a journey and not a destination"*. You need to be able to enjoy this journey.

When there is a problematic behaviour of any sort, it is a bit like sitting in the back of the car with someone else driving it for you. Not only that, they are driving your shiny car down a muddy road. It is not where you want to go, nor how you want it to be.

More importantly, I would argue that the peace, joy and happiness I have seen in the lives of men who have successfully mastered their problem is a jubilant thing to observe; happy, well-functioning men, leading full and productive lives. Oscar Wilde noted *"Be yourself, everyone else is already taken"*. You cannot have somebody else's life, so you must make the most of yours. Therefore bring about the necessary changes as soon as possible.

Another assumption I made when I wrote this book is that while many men will be able to fix this situation themselves, and I would encourage you to do as much of this as possible, some of you will be smart enough to realise that professional help can be beneficial. When my car breaks down I am quite capable of doing some basic mechanics but I would not think twice about taking my car to a service centre to have a specialist fix the problem. If my car is running roughly,

I know enough to know that I have a problem. However, a well-trained mechanic may be able to tell me what the problem is, just from hearing the noise. They apply specialist tools to fix the problem. Therefore, I would encourage you to seek out mental health specialists who can help with your problem through the application of their specialist tools.

Help comes in many different shapes and sizes. There are specially trained psychologists, general counsellors, self-help groups, religious-based groups, addiction recovery programs, 12 step programs and so forth. Some will use methods similar to this book, while others work on a different philosophy. For example, my assumption is that you have a problem which you can ultimately fix. Some of the 12 step programs work on the assumption that you have to admit that the problem is bigger than you, that you are powerless to change and that you will need to hand your power to a higher authority. I believe there is a lot of good work done through such programs and that they help some people. If they work for you, great! But what it means is, if you are working through this book, you need to find ideas which are compatible with all of those who are currently helping you. Therefore, do a little research on some of the assumptions underlying the way in which your specialist or program works and their experience with problems such as yours.

Men coming to therapy often find it an interesting and at times awkward experience. On average, men would like someone to give them a solution – fix it up and away they go. Therapists want people to address emotions by doing a lot of talking, rather than a lot of doing. Many different types of therapy exist because the right therapy really does help. I do encourage you, if you are seeking therapy, to ensure that you feel comfortable with the person and that their methods will work for you. However, just because one person did not fix the problem for you, somebody else may have a different method which does work for you. This means you must seek someone with whom you feel relatively comfortable, and who communicates in a way in which you can relate. I would argue that drawing on the assistance of others is a very helpful part of the recovery process. But at the end of the day, no-one is going to do it for you. It is up to you.

Key Points

- It is important to ensure that you practice the exercises at the end of each section. You will only get back what you put into the process.

- Willpower is not enough to overcome the problem. The more you try to stop a behaviour through willpower, the more entrenched it will become. Rather than pull more, you have to let go of the rope.

- The path is hard but you have to go through this process for those around you and, in particular, for yourself.

- Seek professional help to assist with addressing your problems. Find a compatible therapist and try them out. If one therapist doesn't help, consider trying someone who works in a different way.

- Getting better is up to you – no-one else can do it.

Your Best Friend

You picked up this book because you want to get rid of your pornography problem, because either you or those around you are telling you that viewing pornography is a bad thing to do. However, before you start looking at all the problems viewing pornography is causing in your life, and we will do that later, you have to get something straight. Your pornography problem is your best friend. Did you get that? Let me repeat myself – pornography has become your best friend. This statement is a profound truth but many people have not realised this important truth nor do they want to admit it.

If you do not understand what I am saying, think about this. You choose to spend your free time with it. You stay up late together. You may tell lies to others to protect the secret relationship you have. Many of your life activities have stopped in preference to it. Your life is being is being affected but you cannot give up the relationship the two of you share. That sounds like a pretty important relationship to me.

The first step on your recovery journey is not to say how bad it is. It is to recognise how good it is. I would like you to entertain the thought a little longer. Your pornography problem serves a purpose. All behaviour exists for a reason and a behaviour that occurs frequently must have a strong reason to occur. There is a positive benefit which you draw from being online, whether to escape from your day-to-day problems, manage your anxiety or anger, avoid childhood wounds, or achieve sexual release. This best friend also offers powerful sexual experiences which feel good.

Not all people view pornography for the sexual release but the majority do. However, if it was for sexual release only, then you would not need pornography when in a relationship.

You may have a love/hate relationship with this best friend but, unless you can think about why the behaviour exists and is necessary, it is very difficult to progress and change. Later in the book we will look at this from a behavioural perspective and as a psychological approach. For the moment it is critical to explore the benefits that looking at pornography offers to you. The exercise at the end of this section is of critical importance for starting the recovery process. You must work out the advantages of this behaviour. It has relevance and meaning in your life which must be acknowledged.

For the first exercise I would like you to get to know your friend (see the end of this section for details of the exercise). Allow yourself approximately half an hour to write down all of the different benefits you gain from the behaviour. Once you have constructed a list of those benefits you will be ready to engage in the first challenge for addressing the problem.

If you are religious, this will be confronting to you as your teachings say it is all bad behaviour. The shame or guilt may stop you from seeing the reasons why you might like it. However, you more than anybody else must honestly face the fact that at least a part of you likes it. If you place blame on "temptation by the devil", you will not progress.

The future challenge is to take the list of benefits you identify to seek one or more alternative behaviours necessary to meet the need for those benefits. Therefore, if you have identified that pornography fills a sexual need, then you have to create a healthy, functioning sexual relationship. If you identified escape from stress as a benefit, you need to do some stress management work and identify alternative ways of dealing with stressful situations. If you identified dealing with angry feelings as a benefit, then you need to do some assertiveness and, perhaps, anger management training.

At this stage you do not have to know how to achieve the goal. It is sufficient to begin to realise what you are doing and what else you might need in your life. Letting go of the rope not only releases the monster, it will also release your friend. You need to replace both.

> **Key Points**
>
> - Your pornography problem serves a purpose. All behaviour exists for a reason and a behaviour that occurs frequently must have a strong reason to occur.
>
> - Your pornography problem is like a best friend because you spend a significant part of your life with it. The first step to recovery to is to understand the benefits and payoffs from having such a friend.

Exercise 3 – Benefits and Feelings

Draw two columns on a blank sheet of paper. Head the first column "positive feelings" and the second "benefits". Under each heading list all the examples you can think of. Most people can list at least 10 or more positive feelings.

Setting the Scene 19

The importance here is that for you there are practical payoffs and management of feelings. If you cannot identify feelings that are being managed by the pornography you may need therapy to help you to understand your feelings.

When you have the list, you can begin to use it to develop alternative payoffs and new ways of meeting those feelings. At this stage just have a go at listing some ideas. Later in the book we will do some exercises using the ABC model of behaviour change, and this preliminary material can be used to help in that process.

Exercise 4 – Journal Reflections

Some points to reflect upon include:-

- I have made a provocative statement in saying that your bad behaviour is also a friend. How do you feel about your problem being a "best friend"?

- Do you have any ideas about what you have to do to create a new best friend in your life? How will you fill the void when the Internet pornography has gone?

These may seem like simple questions but they are at the heart of addressing your problem. When you get to the end of this book, you might like to answer these same questions again to see how much your views have changed.

Exercise 5 – Values Exercise

Becoming motivated about what matters most is an important process. I have adapted an exercise from Russ Harris' mindfulness approach to help with this process.

Think about how deep down inside some things are really important to you. What do you want your life to stand for? What sort of qualities as a person do you want to cultivate? What do you want your relationships with others to be like?

Values are the heart's deepest desires for the way in which we want to interact with and relate to the world, other people, and ourselves. They are leading principles that can guide and motivate us as we move through life. Values are not the same as goals. Values are the directions we keep moving in, whereas goals are what we want to achieve along the way.

The following areas of life are those that are valued by some people. Not everyone has the same values and, therefore, this is not a test to see whether you have the "correct" values. Think about each area in terms of general life directions, rather than in terms of specific goals. There may be certain areas that you don't value much; you can skip them if you wish.

1. Family relations. What sort of relationships do you want to have? What personal qualities would you like to bring to those relationships? How would you interact with others if you were the 'ideal you' in these relationships?

2. Marriage/couples/intimate relations. What sort of partner would you like to be in an intimate relationship? What personal qualities would you like to develop? How would

you interact with your partner if you were the 'ideal you' in this relationship?

3. Parenting. What sort of parent would you like to be? What sort of qualities would you like to have? What sort of relationships would you like to build with your children? How would you behave if you were the 'ideal you'?

4. Friendships/social life. If you could be the best friend possible, how would you behave towards your friends? What sort of friendships would you like to build?

5. Career/employment. What do you value in your work? What would make it more meaningful? What kind of worker would you like to be? If you were living up to your own ideal standards, what personal qualities would you like to bring to your work?

6. Education/personal growth and development. What do you value about learning, education, training or personal growth? What new skills would you like to learn? What knowledge would you like to gain?

7. Recreation/fun/leisure. What sorts of hobbies, sports or leisure activities do you enjoy? How do you relax and unwind? How do you have fun? What sorts of activities would you like to do?

8. Spirituality. Spirituality means different things to different people, so whatever spirituality means to you is fine. It may be as simple as communing with nature, or as formal as participation in an organised religious group. What is important to you in this area of life?

9. Citizenship/environment/community life. How would you like to contribute to your community or environment?

10. Health/physical wellbeing. What are your values in relation to maintaining your physical wellbeing? How do you want to look after your health, with regard to sleep, diet, exercise, smoking, alcohol, etc? Why is this important?

If you list the values on a card or sheet, you can refer to the values to keep focussed on them when working through the exercises in this book. These exercises may help to set goals and explore other activities.

2

The Problems

The Internet Addiction Test

The Internet addiction test, developed by Widyanto and McMurren in 2004, was one of the first tests validated for the assessment of Internet addiction. It is not specifically for pornography addiction, but for problematic use of the Internet. I have included the test at the end of this section as it is a good starting point for determining your problem areas in general. When you have completed it, please return to this section to find out what the results mean.

Did you do the test? Good. There are two ways to use the results. The first is to add up the scores on each question to calculate the grand total. The second is to look at any ratings of 4 or 5 against an individual question to identify problem areas. We will go over the total scores below but basically the higher the total score, the greater the level of compulsion.

The normal range is 0 to 30. If you are in this range, congratulations – your computer use is normal. However, if you have a 4 or 5 scored against any of the individual questions look carefully at the item as it indicates a problem. If your score is 30 or below, and no questions scored 4 or 5, I am curious to know the reason why you are reading this book. You do not seem to have the sort of problem which warrants special intervention.

Scores in the 31 to 49 range indicate that a problem may be starting. The Internet may not be out of control but there are a few areas where you may have a problem. Individual scores will show you where the problem lies. The test authors would describe your problem as being in the mild range. The questions that scored a 4 or 5 will determine whether the impact is mild.

If your score is in the 50 to 79 range you are classified as having a moderate problem. To score in this range, you have indicated that many of the items in the questions occur frequently.

If you are still looking for your score, you are in the severe range of problem usage. Scores of 80 to 100 represent a severe problem because you have indicated that most items occur "often" or "always". You probably have so many scores of 4 and 5 that individually they do not provide much further insight.

It is important that you keep your score because in the future you should repeat the test to see how you are progressing. More importantly, as treatment starts to change behaviour, this is one test which will help you to see which areas in your life are currently problematic.

Exercise 6 – Internet Addiction Test

Complete the Internet addiction test. It is best to make a copy as you may want to take it again later to see how you are progressing and to help identify problem areas.

Simply answer the 20 items below on a five-point rating scale.

0 = not applicable   3 = frequently

1 = rarely   4 = often

2 = occasionally   5 = always

You should consider only the time spent online for non-academic or non-job purposes when answering. That is, you should consider only recreational use of the Internet.

1. How often do you find that you stay online longer than you intended?	
2. How often do you neglect household chores to spend more time online?	
3. How often do you prefer the excitement of the Internet to intimacy with your partner?	
4. How often do you form new relationships with fellow online users?	
5. How often do others in your life complain to you about the amount of time you spend online?	
6. How often do your grades or schoolwork suffer because of the amount of time you spend online?	

7. How often do you check your email before doing something else that you need to do?	
8. How often does your job performance or productivity suffer because of the Internet?	
9. How often do you become defensive or secretive when someone asks you what you do online?	
10. How often do you block out disturbing thoughts about your life with soothing thoughts of the Internet?	
11. How often do you find yourself anticipating when you will go online again?	
12. How often do you fear that life without the Internet would be boring, empty and joyless?	
13. How often do you snap, yell or act annoyed if someone bothers you while you are online?	
14. How often do you lose sleep due to late night log-ins?	
15. How often do you feel preoccupied with the Internet when offline, or fantasise about being online?	
16. How often do you find yourself saying "Just a few more minutes" when online?	
17. How often do you try to cut down the amount of time you spend online and fail?	
18. How often do you try to hide how long you've been online?	
19. How often do you choose to spend more time online over going out with others?	
20. How often do you feel depressed, moody, or nervous when you are offline (which goes away once you are back online)?	

What's My Problem?

As I said in the introduction, all of you are different, and problem behaviour will manifest itself in different aspects of your lives. This early step of your journey is to try and identify the areas of your life that are being impacted upon.

The main reference used by psychologists to classify mental health issues is the Diagnostic and Statistical Manual of the American Psychiatric Association; or DSM. The DSM's fifth edition (the DSM V) classifies Internet pornography problems as a compulsive - impulsive spectrum disorder (hypersexual disorder - pornography) with two main characteristics. The first characteristic is excessive preoccupation with pornography which entails spending too much time thinking about pornography and too much time viewing it. Your score on the Internet Addiction Test completed in Exercise 5 will indicate whether excessive use of the Internet is a problem. The second set of characteristics in the DSM V is that there are problems that are impairing your social life and occupation, and may be causing other negative repercussions in your life.

Social impairment means that you are spending less time in the real world and more time in the cyber world. As a result, when computer time is not available, you may experience mood-related feelings such as anger, depression and tension. Use may include tolerance, meaning that you seek better and faster equipment, and need longer hours for that use. Negative repercussions affecting your life include arguments about excessive use of the Internet, feelings of social isolation, withdrawal from activities, and fatigue.

While these concepts are useful, I would like to categorise the problems in a different way. I would like you to answer the questions at the end of this section (Exercise 6 – Porn Problem Identification). There are only 13 questions and all you have to do is tick the box "yes" if it applies to you. While I am sure I do not need to say this to you, please remember that you can only help yourself to the degree to which you are honest with yourself. These exercises are for your understanding, so please be candid. Go and complete Exercise 6.

Thank you for your honesty in completing Exercise 6. Now we will look at your answers and discuss each of the question sets to help you understand which areas of your life are problematic. This will help you to prioritise the treatment aspects in the latter part of this book.

The analysis is simple. There are 4 sets of questions. Questions 1, 2 and 3 relate to the compulsive nature of your behaviour. Positive answers to questions 4, 5 and 6 indicate that there are problems in your life at a relationship or sexual level. Questions 7, 8 and 9 indicate that your problem is affecting your honesty and moral integrity. Questions 10, 11, 12 and 13 indicate that your problem is so far out of control that it is compromising your legal standing within society.

If you have not answered "yes" to any of the questions in a particular group, then please just skim read the related section to ensure that there are not some aspects of relevance to your life which the questions failed to identify. If you have answered "yes" to all of the questions in a group, you will need to read the relevant section very carefully, as it means that this is a significant problem area for you.

Each question will be discussed with a degree of detail to help you to understand some of the consequences of your problem.

Exercise 7 – Porn Problem Identification

Please tick the "yes" column against the following questions if you think that this might be a problem for you. After completing this checklist go to the related section for a discussion of the results.

	Yes	No
1. Do you say to yourself or others that you will stop viewing Internet pornography but keep doing it anyway?		
2. In the last 2 weeks have you stayed up more than 2 hours beyond your usual bedtime looking at pornography?		
3. Are you seeking harder images for stimulation?		
4. Is your partner disgusted by your behaviour?		
5. Have you been unable to perform sexually with your partner because of recent masturbation to pornography?		
6. Would you rather masturbate to pornography than be with a real partner?		
7. Do you ever lie to cover up your actions, for example, "I was working on a project", "A virus must have downloaded the images", "It was a pop-up", or use some other lie?		
8. Do you ever feel shame or guilt about what you are doing?		

9. Are you religious and view pornography despite your beliefs?		
10. Because of excessive viewing have you ever sought out someone to act upon the behaviour in real time?		
11. Have you had embarrassing moments or near misses, such as being caught looking at pornography at work, or your children seeing your computer images?		
12. Do you ever look at child pornography?		
13. Are there images on your computer which the police could charge you for possessing? Is there material which is so obscene others would be revolted?		

Compulsive Nature

Did you answer "yes" to questions 1, 2 or 3 of the Pornography Problem Identification? If so, you can read more about the compulsive nature of the problem in detail in this section. If not, please just skim read this section to ensure you are not missing something.

The compulsive nature of the problem is one of the defining criteria of a pornography problem. This means that you feel compelled to go online. Even when a part of you says that you should not do it, you do it anyway. As a result, your use of time is very poor. We know from some research studies that as many as 96% of people in treatment identified time management issues as one of the most difficult problems to manage. The nature of a compulsive problem is that it controls your use of time rather than the other way around.

The Internet Addiction Test will have helped you to see that you have a compulsive aspect to your online behaviour, however, that test is not specifically designed for pornography problems. Let us look at the questions related to pornography problem identification in more detail.

Question 1. Irrespective of the definition of a compulsive behaviour, you say that you will stop but you keep doing it anyway. If you have answered "yes" to this item then, if for no other reason, this book is necessary for you. You are showing signs of being out of control, and you are being controlled by the problem instead of the other way around. You want to be the one in the driver's seat controlling your life, not having your life determined by your problems.

Question 2 looks at one of the very common aspects of Internet behaviour; that is, staying up longer than normal bedtime. In the privacy of your own home, especially if you have a family who have all gone to bed, it is easy to look at Internet pornography. Many people look at pornography in work time (which is another indicator of the problem), but late nights on the computer at home makes perfect sense. If you only need to look for 5 or 10 or 15 minutes, getting time alone is not likely to be a problem. But many of the men I see have been on the Internet for 2, 3 or 4 hours beyond the time they would normally go to bed. Some men have a pattern of staying up on weekends for all night binges!

If you want a reality check, the DSM V classification of your problem indicates that it can be a mild, moderate or severe condition. The person who reports that time consumed by fantasies and urges is between 30 minutes and 2 hours per day on an average day is classed as moderate; the person who reports that the time consumed by hypersexual disorder fantasies and urges is more than 2 hours on an average day is classed as having a severe problem. Note that this is not just about the time spent online but also the time spent reflecting on what was seen, or time spent planning to go online again. Almost all of the men I see are in the severe range – while two hours online is nothing, they think about it all day!

There are a number of costs associated with long periods on the Internet, especially at night. Problems associated with sleep deprivation are quite significant. The first of those is a decline in work performance. If you are employed, you will start to jeopardise your employment. If a student, your studies will suffer. If you are self-employed, you might react badly to clients.

There are also secondary effects arising from sleep deprivation. Research shows that the body is under increased levels of stress hormones while sleep deprived, making it more prone to sickness and illness. There is also a debate in the literature in relation to whether or not sleep deprivation is a cause of depression. When this behaviour occurs night after night, and especially on weeknights, it is indicative of a marked impact on a life. Stopping sleep deprivation can make a lot of people feel better emotionally.

Moodiness, irritability and other reactions associated with sleep deprivation are likely to impact upon your relationships. Questions 4 to 6 examine some of the direct impacts on relationships, but the moodiness and irritability associated with sleep deprivation is going to indirectly affect relationships as well.

Another way of framing the same question could have been: *"How much of your spare time is encroached upon by looking at the Internet?"* My experience is that by the time men come into treatment, they have given up many of their activities because they are either too tired or they use all of their spare time on the computer. In effect, they have lost their social life and have taken on a virtual life (elsewhere we will discuss in detail how to rebuild a life outside of the Internet).

Question 3 relates to habituation of stimuli. This piece of fancy psychological jargon simply means that, for some people, images which were arousing to start with lose their impact over time. The substance abuse literature talks about tolerance for the same process.

There are two choices when habituation occurs. One is to seek new, similar images which have an arousal effect. The second is to seek increasingly harder images (either in content, such as from soft to hard-core; or in the means of delivery, such as going from pictures to videos to real life). I see some people who maintain the same level of images for years, but I also see men who escalate. The problem with escalation is that it increasingly requires more and more graphic images which impact on a person's sense of self, and relationships with others, because the reality is altered.

As will be discussed a little later in this book, technology has also enabled exposure to images to become more intense because of the quantity of material available. Originally people looked at pictures. Now movies are easily and readily available. Movies have more and more graphic content. Therefore there is an ever-increasing smorgasbord designed to appeal. The content is tailored, harder core graphic material, which is available more frequently and in greater amounts.

For some men habituation is linked to some types of legal problems. I have seen men who are attracted to child pornography because they are interested in children, but I have also seen a number of men who have drifted from normal heterosexual interests with adult women, to teen, young teen and then early adolescent content because the images have a greater arousal pull (due to the associated taboos). Over the passage of time some men then become hooked on material which is illegal.

Another variation of the same process relates to men with religious backgrounds who start off looking at underwear on lingerie sites or in shop catalogues and through other legally available sources, but who gradually drift into harder and harder images, and in the process become more and more disgusted with themselves.

As indicated, gradual habituation to harder images does not occur for everyone, but for those for whom it is occurring, it becomes an increasing problem. Often people who have a more extrovert nature are more inclined to habituate quickly, as they are seeking constant excitement and become bored easily. However, they are not the only ones who will do it as almost everyone will seek new images and more arousing material. It is a relatively normal behavioural process but with serious consequences.

There are many other ways in which the compulsive aspect of the behaviour can impact upon lives. The starting proposition is that if you have answered "yes" to some of these questions, your life is out of control and you need control strategies.

Key Points

- Pornography problems are compulsive patterns of behaviour which interfere with normal functioning.

- Internet pornography problems are classified as a compulsive - impulsive spectrum disorder with four main characteristics: excessive use of the Internet; withdrawal, tolerance, and negative repercussions in life.

- Sleep deprivation associated with late nights will take its toll on your physical health, mental health, work performance and relationships. You need sleep to function well.

- Some of you will find image excitement habituates so you will seek either new images or harder images for renewed excitement. While extraverts are more prone to this pattern, all users experience seeking new images for arousal purposes.

Exercise 8 – Journal Reflections

What impacts on your life can you see from being controlled by pornography? Make a list of problems which need to be addressed. Some of these will be covered later in the book, while you may need to research some strategies to address other problems. For example, there is a large amount of literature on treating depression or improving sleep hygiene.

Damaging Relationships

Did you answer "yes" to questions 4, 5 or 6 of the Pornography Problem Identification? If so, read this section to begin to understand the impact of your problems on the relationships which matter most in your life, particularly your relationship with your partner. If you have no relationship, it is still worth a quick read to foresee what may happen.

This second set of questions from the Pornography Problem Identification questionnaire relate to personal and sexual relationships. A number of you who read this book might be single. You might be young and looking for a first partner, older but never married, or have been married and are now divorced or widowed. However, my typical younger client in his early twenties may not have had a relationship when the pornography problem started (he used the Internet to fill his sexual needs) but, when he enters a relationship, he finds that his pornography problem does not suddenly disappear when he has a sexual outlet. He finds the opposite, as he struggles to fulfil the new partner with limited resources, that is, due to his night-time activities and his distorted view of sexuality. Young women complain that partners have sex without affection, due to their partners acting out what they have seen on the Internet.

In older clients who are married, I often see an increase in relationship-related issues when their use of pornography becomes problematic. One of the most common referrals I see is when a wife or girlfriend finds out that their husband or partner is choosing to use pornography when they are supposed to be in a relationship.

Pornography for some people becomes a means of relieving sexual tension both with and without a relationship. This book is written for those of you who may have both moral (usually religious) beliefs against pornography, and for those of you who accept pornography as a useful and acceptable part of life. I want to offer help rather than a moral judgement about either philosophy of pornography use. It is important that I work within your framework. However, what I want to point out is that when the behaviour reaches a point where it interferes with normal relationships, then it is a problem for any man, whether or not he has a moral issue with masturbating to pornography.

Beginning with Question 4, the questionnaire raises the point that partners can be disgusted by the behaviour. I have included a section on partners' reactions later in the book, because women in relationships often see pornography very differently from men. Some of the women I have seen feel a sense of betrayal, as if their partner were having an affair, or see their partner in a negative or reprehensive light because of their partner's actions. If your behaviour is impacting upon your partner such that she feels disgusted or repulsed by the things you are doing, you have a problem. Your relationship should be a place of support. However, if your partner, rather than being a support, is strongly opposed to the things you are doing, the impacts of that are going to make your life terrible. A happy relationship is one of the best places on earth, but the opposite is true – a bad relationship is hell on earth.

I have seen men who have used pornography for years as a single person without it being a problem for them. The problems arose when they entered a relationship, due to their

The Problems 39

partner's reaction. As will be discussed later in the book, pornography creates a false sense of what sexual encounters are like and that can have a negative impact on relationships because women feel objectified rather than intimate. If you want a healthy relationship, then it is critical that your sexual relationship is able to function, and that each of you views the other with wholesome respect.

In my experience, one of the most common reasons men come to therapy is that their partners want them to. This makes it harder to treat those men because the motivation is really another person's but, because they value their relationships, they do come to therapy. If you are reading this book because your partner wants you to fix the problem, at some point you need to accept that you have to want to fix it for yourself, even if that is just to keep your relationship.

Question 5 relates to being unable to perform with a partner due to recent masturbation. We know that approximately 75% of online pornography users find that their sexual performance diminishes as a result of their pornography problem. It is likely to be a significant issue for you. Some men use excuses such as improving their sex lives, or teaching themselves sexuality to justify looking at pornography. However, because they are going on the Internet night after night, they have nothing left to give their partner at an intimate level. Sexuality is an important part of a healthy relationship and, unless this factor is addressed, the relationship is seriously at risk.

Question 6 relates to the fact that for some men the fantasies they create in their head become more satisfying than the relationship with their partner. There are a number of reasons why this can happen. It may be because of problems, sometimes longstanding, in relating sexually to a partner, but it can also relate to the fact that fantasies are easy and immediately available, avoiding the need to deal with intimacy and relationship issues. My argument is simple – it is a very unhealthy state to be in. If your preference is for images rather than a real person, this is a problem that needs to be addressed.

Unless you address these issues to enable you to have a healthy, functioning sex life, and/or if you answered "yes" to any of these questions, you have some work to do on your sexuality, intimacy or relationship with your partner.

Key Points

- Many intimate relationships are damaged by excessive use of pornography by one of the partners in that relationship.

- For most men, sexual functioning with their partner decreases with excessive pornography viewing.

- Partners may feel like objects rather than equals when sexual activity is coloured by unreal perceptions of sexuality.

Exercise 9 – Listing the Impacts upon your Relationship

Draw a line in the middle of a page. On the left make a list of all the impacts your problem has had on your intimacy and sexual relationship. On the right, list possible actions you could take to help fix these problems.

Moral Integrity

Did you answer "yes" to questions 7, 8 or 9 of the Pornography Problem Identification? If so, read the following information about the impact on your sense of morality, honesty and sense of self. If not, please just skim read this section.

A story told in different forms concerns a young native American brave who, as he approaches early manhood and is plagued by bad thoughts, seeks the advice of one of the elders. The elder explains that within everybody there are two dogs (wolves) fighting one another: one dog that does good things, and another dog that desires to do bad things. Curious, the young man then asks *"which dog wins?"* The wise Elder explains *"the one you feed the most"*.

When you engage in a behaviour that you keep private, the problem is that you feed the wrong dog. To protect yourself from being discovered, you engage in actions and excuses to hide the fact that you are doing things which others would find reprehensible or repulsive. Therefore, you make excuses and lie about what you are doing. Over time this begins to affect your moral character where the public self and the private self are at odds with each other. This creates a terrible internal dilemma, often associated with feelings of shame, guilt, disgust and revulsion.

Question 7 relates to the fact that you have to cover your tracks; you tell lies and make excuses as to why behaviours and explanations are inconsistent. Lying to a spouse, colleagues, workmates and so forth, while serving a protective function, gradually generates shame. The more the behaviour takes place, the more there will be near misses as someone finds you doing something embarrassing, and the more you then have to cover your behaviour. Most people in recovery who have answered similarly to these items note how good it feels when they progress to the point where their actions internally and externally are consistent and they no longer need to make excuses.

Question 8 is largely a direct consequence of question 7. If you are doing things which are wrong and are hiding them – and you still have a conscience – there has to be some sense of shame. This internal inconsistency in psychology has been called an ego-dystonic behaviour. What this means is that a set of behaviours is inconsistent with the sense of self. For some people, looking at pornography causes them no sense of shame or guilt and they do not have to lie about it (called "ego-syntonic"). But for others this is a problem. Ultimately, to feel good about yourself, this dilemma has to be resolved. There are only a few ways to resolve it. The first is to go public about the behaviour because you no longer care, or find a way to rationalise it so that you lose the guilt making it no longer internally inconsistent. Another way is to eliminate the shame-generating behaviour from your life.

Question 9 refers to the spiritual and religious dilemmas which can be generated by viewing pornography. Later in the book I devote a section to religious issues. I readily accept that some of you have no belief in God and that this might not be an issue for you. However, for those of you who belong to a religion which strongly condemns the use of pornography, the sense of shame is profound. Looking upon women for lust is a major sin in many religions.

As will be explained in more detail later, I believe it is important that you seek good spiritual counsel. I have seen a number of people from different religions who have an added level of shame created by a misinterpretation of what their religion says. I would strongly suggest making sure that you speak to appropriate leaders for spiritual assistance. However, it is important that you find somebody supportive. Some religious leaders, because of their own beliefs, simply condemn and shame without providing support and direction. Saying *"stop it or you will go to hell"* offers no practical help when the compulsion is driving the control. It adds guilt which makes someone desire to escape. As you will see in a later section, this is the very mechanism which drives the problem.

In any church with which I have dealt, there are always some leaders who understand that the sin and the sinner are separate. Others seem unable to separate behaviours from the person. You need to ensure that your religious leaders can support you as a person, even though they may condemn your actions. You do not need someone condemning you as a person for a behaviour you are struggling to master. If you are religious, there are some specific tools to assist you later in the book.

Key Points

- It is normal to not want someone to know that you are looking at pornography. However, each time you cover your tracks or lie, you are selling out your integrity and self-worth.

- When behaviours are inconsistent with your sense of self (ego-dystonic), you are generating an internal emotional struggle. You gradually give up your values or damage your sense of self unless you change the behaviour or how you view the problem.

- Religious conflicts are very significant problems for those of you who have both a faith and a pornography problem.

- Seek counsel from leaders who understand the issues and can help you to feel worthwhile. They need to love the sinner but hate the sin.

- You may have forgotten how good it feels, but having a life where what you do in private and public is the same will mean no more lies or excuses. You will feel wonderful.

Exercise 10 – Journal Reflections

Write about the impact pornography has had on your sense of self. How would it feel to not have to worry about being caught out doing something which could be shameful or embarrassing?

Illegal and Dangerous Acts

Whether or not you answered "yes" to questions 10, 11, 12 or 13 of the Pornography Problem Identification you should, for your own safety, read about the legal and dangerous aspects. Some people do not even realise that they have been committing an illegal act until it is too late!

My starting proposition is that many of you who view Internet pornography are never tempted to seek out material which society defines as offensive, illegal or inappropriate – nor do you necessarily seek to act it out with a real person. If there was a direct link between looking at pornography and acting out sexually with real people then there would be rapidly escalating rates of sexual acting out (as the number of viewers are increasing exponentially). This does not appear to be the case.

If you have answered "yes" to any of these questions, you are putting yourself at very serious risk of significant consequences. Engaging in dangerous and illegal activities can be devastating to your future, while sexual acting out can endanger your life, health and relationships.

Question 10 concerns how, if you watch something often enough, you may want to actually do it. A case in point was a man in his mid-twenties who was referred to me for chronic anxiety. When I saw him in my office, the source of his anxiety was that he had become interested and excited by transsexual pornography. He had repeatedly viewed images and had a desire to experience it. Even though he was in a long-term heterosexual relationship, he organised a trip to Bali and had paid sex with a transsexual street worker.

The source of anxiety was when his rational mind kicked in and he realised that approximately 10% of sex workers in that part of the world suffer from HIV. He spent a very nervous six months waiting for his final test results.

Similarly, I have seen a religious man who, while his wife was at work, acted out with prostitutes in the family home. One of the women he paid for sex returned at a time when his wife was home and demanded more money. The wife was devastated and left with the children. I saw another man who was seriously bashed and robbed when he thought he was meeting a woman for a casual encounter based on sexual fantasies he had viewed on the Internet. The encounter was in fact set up by a couple of male drug addicts who wanted to rob someone. He was not willing to go to the police as he was in a socially important position, so they got away with it.

I am not saying that simply looking will cause you to act, but thought precedes action, repetitive thought tends to desensitise, and repetitive viewing heightens the desire for such actions. A desire to experiment or act out fantasies which are being created by the Internet, especially when they are against your normal views and values, is the mark of a very serious progression in your problem. If you are engaging in risky or dangerous practices you are putting yourself and those around you at risk.

Question 11 refers to some of the near misses you could have when engaging in the problem at inappropriate times, such as having pornography on the computer which children could see, or viewing images at work. While I have framed the question along the lines of embarrassment, what some people do not realise is that these acts can also be illegal.

The Problems 47

It is possible in many parts of the world to be fired from employment for viewing pornography during work time, even if the pornography is not actually of an illegal nature. Similarly, I have been involved in care and protection matters where parents have had children removed if the children have been exposed to pornography.

Questions 12 and 13 relate to child pornography and storing images on the computer which are classified by society as obscene. Many societies have laws against having obscene images, for example images of sexual encounters with animals. You may have had some of those images for "fun", but you may not necessarily realise that you are potentially committing criminal offences which can result in a conviction and jail term.

Child pornography quite rightly is seen in a very serious light in many parts of the world. Hopefully one day all of the world will understand the damage caused by the sexual abuse of children. Where child pornography is illegal it often results in jail sentences and, in some parts of the western world, it also results in people being placed on sex offender registers. For example, in Australia, it is possible to end up on a sex offender register for 7 to 12 years (meaning that the police can come into your house or workplace at any time of the day or night and view your computer and search your house for pornographic images). If this happens to you it would be completely devastating to your life and future.

Depending on the wording of the criminal offence provision, accessing or possessing explicit stories describing children engaging in sexual activities (even if there are no pictures or illustrations) can be illegal. Similarly, I prepared a pre-sentence report for a man who had only viewed cartoon child pornography (that is, not real children). He didn't think the cartoon images would be illegal. Unfortunately for him the offence provision also prohibited material that depicted a child or a representation of a child.

A final point is that in a world of cheap commercial travel, the material you have on your computer or phone may be acceptable in your home country, however, the images may actually be illegal in another country. Therefore be careful about any material stored on your electronic equipment.

> **Key Points**
>
> - Shame and guilt result when your actions have to be kept hidden from others. This will eat away at your sense of self if you have a public face different to your inner world.
>
> - Recognise and seek help if you are dealing with matters which are illegal or dangerous.
>
> - There are severe legal consequences for material deemed offensive, exploitive, or involving child pornography. Do not risk the consequences as people do get caught and when they do the results can be devastating.

Exercise 11 – Action Time

Is there anything illegal in your collection which needs to be addressed? See later sections of this book for instructions on what to do about this.

3
Facts and Information

Some Facts about Pornography

Men like facts. To give you some facts about your problem, I will briefly review the history of pornography and then explain how these societal changes can impact on your brain. You will then be able to find out where you fit in the scheme of things. The critical point is that there is a merging of two different factors. One factor is that pornography has been around in many societies for a long time, making it a part of life. The other factor is that technology is creating more opportunities to view pornography.

One of the earliest forms of pornography is found in ancient caves in different parts of the world. There is a variety of art in caves, but two sorts of images are often depicted – feats of daily life, such as killing animals, and pictures related to sexuality and fertility. For example, in ancient India, there was a mixing of sexual and fertility images in pottery, pictures and sculpture. Books like the *Kama Sutra*, created in India around 1500 years ago, were explicit manuals on sexuality. On a tour of Pompeii, a city destroyed by volcanic ash in AD 79, our tour guide indicated that the grand highlight of the tour was the phallic images in the streets showing the way to the brothel. The brothel contained images of a pornographic nature depicting various sexual acts.

Sexuality, sexual images, fertility and religion have intermingled in most societies. However, sharing images was previously a problem. You had to go to the cave or building to see the images. Books like the Kama Sutra were hand drawn works of art, rather than mass produced copies, limiting their availability. Furthermore, the images were not real people but copies or caricatures of real people. It is also difficult to know how much the images were used to arouse (which is what pornography does) and how much was a statement of life. Kama Sutra and Pompeii clearly concerned sexual images for sexual purposes.

The industrial revolution enabled the situation to change in two significant ways; images became increasingly portable and shareable, and images of real people engaging in real acts became possible. In the early 1800s the daguerreotype became the first commercially available means of photography. This forerunner to the camera consisted of chemical plates which could capture images. It did not take very long after the technology was developed before people started taking "naughty" pictures, of which approximately 800 are still in existence from that era. From these early beginnings, plate images evolved into photography which became easier, cheaper and more shareable. Nude photography became possible and, like all new technology, photography was quickly used for this purpose.

Amazing technological advances produced motion pictures, the forerunner of today's movies. Real people could be filmed while engaging in actions rather than remaining in a passive pose. Of course this then opened up a moral debate for society. Mainstream movies created a scandal when, in around 1896, the first risqué publically shown movie called 'The Kiss', was seen. The scandal resulted in the movie being banned for a period of time because it showed kissing. A kiss shown publically in today's western society is seen as completely mundane, but 120 years ago it was scandalous.

In the 1940s, soldiers had pin-up pictures of women either clad in underwear or partially nude, but it was only in 1953 that Hugh Hefner started Playboy Magazine (and that organisation was almost bankrupt at the time of writing because of changing social times). This was the start of modern pornography for the masses.

In 1970 Penthouse magazine showed pubic hair for the first time. Over time more and more has been allowed to be revealed and now most modern porn stars don't even have pubic hair to show! These magazines, coupled with changing social values, created an era of socially acceptable pornography. Books for adult readers were often available at service stations or newsagents. This material was loosely defined as "soft-core", and it was generally considered to be socially acceptable for adults to view it. Many of my male clients in their 40s and 50s viewed soft porn (often hidden in their father's briefcase or office) as teenagers when their sexuality was emerging.

A second level of material appeared in parallel to "softcore" pornography. It was available through informal and sometimes illegal means – the so called "hard-core" pornography. The black market for pornographic material has existed but often hidden on the fringes of society. As values changed further, adult shops emerged to sell the harder core material. However, even though availability increased, there were a number of difficulties in procuring such material. A person had to drive to the shop during business hours and risk being seen by others. They then had to purchase material from a real person, and leave the shop without being seen. All of this was a barrier and a limit to how much material could be consumed.

The technical revolution created another level of technology essential to sow the seeds for the current pornography tidal wave. The video recorder – what seems like dinosaur technology in an age of DVDs and Blu Ray – did something very important. It allowed movies to be copied easily without the need for a laboratory to develop the film. Not only could material of a harder nature be easily shared, people could from that point onward create their own movies.

The final aspect of this explosion in technology was the advent of the computer, the creation of the worldwide web, and the ability to share movies without making a physical copy. These factors have been the catalyst for the current tsunami of images. The Internet has been the vehicle which has facilitated the availability of pornography on an unprecedented scale. As an undergraduate, and then in my early career, I learned of sexual problems related to images viewed on an occasional basis (usually either fetishes or child pornography). Now the Internet has allowed tens of thousands and probably millions of otherwise normal men to become slaves to computer pornography.

The Internet as a medium is absolutely fascinating. The Internet began in the late 1960s as the ARPANET (the Advanced Research Projects Agency Network), initially supported by the US Department of Defense and then by the US National Science Foundation in the 1980s. The Internet started to reach other countries in the late 1980s and really spread its reach, and became more public, during the 1990s. At the time of writing this book, it has taken just three decades for the Internet to become an integral part of our life. Where the development of the Internet takes us in the future will be an incredible journey.

As soon as the Internet was up and running, the sharing of pornographic pictures started. The problem was that it was slow to transfer picture images. Broadband was not available until the early 2000s, at which point the higher speed allowed for the sharing of movies to become a viable option.

The reason why the technology is so important for a pornography problem has to do with download speeds. In the days of dial up access, if you wanted a twenty second movie clip of moderate quality you would have to sit and wait for the download, during which time (approximately two or three minutes) the computer was not available for anything else. After finishing the download, another movie could be located and downloaded. With basic broadband, it can take just sixteen seconds to download a movie (and you could probably continuing searching, albeit more slowly, while it was downloading). With the higher speeds of advanced cable broadband the same short movie can take less than two seconds to download, during which it's possible to search for other movies. Therefore, more material can be downloaded more quickly than ever before.

In addition to the sharing of pornography, there are now social networking sites (like Facebook), user groups and dating sites. Material can be shared among Internet users from all over the world. On a social level something like 30% of all new relationships start via the Internet, not to mention that it is now used to meet people for sexual encounters. YouTube equivalents have also created a revolution in the porn world in that people can now upload their own amateur movies.

The amount of pornography is amassing rapidly. Old movies are converted to computer formats and made available on the Internet. New movies are created by movie industries in different parts of the world, and people are uploading their homemade versions. New sites are created daily so the sheer volume of pornography which can be found and downloaded onto a computer is really quite amazing. As the material is rarely removed, it simply adds to the quantity available. For example, in 2007 I typed the word "sex" in a Google search and retrieved 761 million items. Four years later, I used the same word in a Google search and retrieved a massive 1,960 million items. When I searched for the word "porn", there was a quarter of a billion items in 2007 and 875 million items four years later.

The quantity of material is massive. There are questionable estimates which indicate that 52 million unique pornography sites exist. It is also estimated that between 100 and 2500 new pornographic sites are created each week. Whatever the real figures are, there an incredible number of sites.

Many of them are slight variations of an original site, often with the same material. Why are new pornographic sites created each week? It helps to bypass Internet filters which screen for sites in different ways, including screening by known site names. A new site can exist for a while before it makes the banned list. The creation of new sites also allows for habituation. The pornography sellers know that you want variety. The designers recreate the same site to overcome the filters which filter by website names. Similarly, if you are looking for new or novel material, you will be more interested in looking at a new site. As any Internet pornography user knows, the new sites link to other sites.

Technology allows for very precise marketing. The site owners can review which images are viewed and for how long. They can then readjust the site to make it more appealing. Once you are viewing the site the site owners use clever marketing devices. While many of the people I see do not use pay sites, the free sites are not a community service but a way of enticing users to pay. They provide short or low quality samples, or create frustration by linking you to other sites, or advertise pay sites. They have enticing offers, such as paying only $1 for a three day trial, only to find restrictions in what can be downloaded. I need not say too much more other than to make the point that technology and advanced marketing means the sites are as appealing as possible making it psychologically hard to avoid looking further once you start.

For you, the pornography user, the implications of these social and technological revolutions are tremendous. The practical barriers which previously put a layer of protection between you and the material are gone. The social rules have changed as there are no moral standards on the Internet. The volume of material is incomprehensible, but most significantly the material can appealingly packaged and delivered to you 24 hours a day, 7 days a week. The problem for you is that, when you try to give up, relapse is just seconds away. If bored with an image, there are a million new ones on the next search. If you had to drive to a bookstore to buy a book or movie, not only would get bored with the material, you would probably only do it occasionally.

There are no restrictions on the type of material you can see – you can see anything at all, and I mean anything. There is nothing of a sexual nature that I can think of which is not available. Most of the men I see in therapy are viewing things that ten years ago they would not have even thought people could do!

I have included this historical overview to highlight an important point. Historically, there were barriers which added layers of protection between you and the pornography. These practical and social barriers have been drastically eroded, which, when coupled with the technological sophistication of the Internet, means that the only real protection left is self-control.

In my opinion, when applied to the Internet, any previous arguments about acceptable types of pornography have gone.

Facts and Information

The sophisticated marketing developed on the Internet's advanced technology, coupled with an increasing volume of material, represents a modern plague for society. Like a plague, some people are not infected, others are exposed but do not get sick, but for those who do become infected, the sickness is severe and reinfection is at toxic levels. As I see it, there is no immunity, just avoidance of the infection in the first place.

> **Key Points**
>
> - Pornography has been a part of many societies but historically in fairly limited and restricted amounts. Social rules have also restricted the way which the material was shared.
>
> - The sharing of pornography has historically been difficult due to the nature of the technology used – for example, hard copies had to be passed person to person – but, with improvements to Internet technology, material can be shared without limits.
>
> - With the removal of practical, social and moral limits which historically restricted the sharing of material, the only remaining restriction is self-control.
>
> - Sophisticated marketing developed on the Internet's advanced technology, coupled with an increasing volume of material, represents a modern plague for society. There is no immunity, so avoidance of infection is ultimately the best strategy.

Exercise 12 – Journal Reflections

- How has changing technology impacted upon your pornography problem?

- Are you a victim of marketing strategies?

- What have you learnt about the way in which you might be manipulated by advertisers of pornography?

What is Common?

When you meet a friend who asks you *"what did you do last night?"*, you will readily tell them about watching a sporting event or a television program, or that you were working on a work project or school assignment. Relatively few of you will say *"I saw some great porn last night"*, other than to really close friends. It is estimated that 70% of porn site visitors keep their activities a secret. In other words, it is not something that is discussed openly and therefore you will not know what is going on in the lives of other men.

Even if you were someone in that 30% who do talk to a close friend about your activities, you probably won't tell anyone that you were masturbating to the pornography. Why? Sexuality is generally a private thing and one of the least spoken about aspects of human behaviour. Paradoxically, sexual jokes are common. Therefore, the information people share is usually superficially funny comments, which are inaccurate, demeaning or myth-based. People struggle to discuss serious issues in a meaningful manner.

Therefore I will provide some comments about what is common, because if you have never discussed what others do you will not have a frame of reference with which to compare your behaviour. Knowledge of the problem can help you to get past the shame and embarrassment and get on with the task of dealing with the problem.

The first point I would make is that there no such thing as *"normal"* pornography viewing. A religious person may believe that no pornography is acceptable, while someone of a secular background may not have any concerns about viewing highly explicit material. In science there is no moral judgement about right and wrong, in society there is *"political correctness"*, in religion absolute judgement, and in the lives of individuals the right to choose. I have strong personal opinions about what I consider to be morally wrong, but in this book I put my views aside, at least in part. I am not trying to be politically correct, and this is not the forum for a religious debate. I will add separate comment for those of you who hold religious views as I know that you will have a special struggle in this regard. What I want to do as much as possible is to explain the issues and provide some tools for your consideration. That is why you have chosen this book, so that you, a unique individual, can get the tools to help.

With respect to the viewing of pornography, there has been some research into what people view. Having some idea of what is happening in society can help provide benchmarks in understanding the underlying psychological dynamics. I find many men are greatly relieved to find out they are not alone with this problem.

An interesting book on the frequency and use of pornography in Australia is the *'Porn Report'* by McGee, Aubrey and Lumbey (Melbourne University Press). In 2008 the authors surveyed the types of movies being looked at and the types of movie scenes being viewed, and explored other issues such as magazines versus the Internet. It is a snapshot which helps to describe what was common in the Australian community at the time their book was written.

I qualify the examples cited below with the point that the nature of pornography viewing, and the whole porn industry, is changing rapidly with technological change.

I suspect that the figures on the way people view pornography will have changed, in the same way that everything in society changes. A simple example is the Yellow Pages phone book. Until approximately 5 years ago, I used the Yellow Pages to find all of the businesses I needed. I have not picked up a hard copy Yellow Pages for several years, using instead the Yellow Pages online. In this example, I engage in the same behaviour using a different medium. However, I often use an Internet search engine to find a business, that is, I use a new method to do the same task. I believe it is the same with pornography – some of what is happening online is the same as before, but there are also new viewing methods emerging.

Some statistics from the Porn Report help to put into perspective what is happening in the community. The first statistic is that 33% of Australian adults used some kind of sexually explicit material. As would be expected, 82% of those people were male. If we consider both figures it means that about 27% of men are admitting to viewing pornography at some time.

The Porn Report shows that the vast majority, but not all, of the women who looked at pornography were looking at it with their partners. Only a very small percentage of women were looking at it in their own right. When I ran a workshop in 2004, the information available indicated that women were not interested in visual images at all. Since then, particularly with the Internet, the research indicates that there is an increasing number of women who look at images. Some recent research found that as many as one in three visitors to a porn site was a woman. Future research may well show that an increasing number of women are viewing images. Having said that, for reasons described later in the book, I think that due to fundamental differences between the genders it is unlikely that it will become as high a frequency occurrence for women as it is for men, and I am of the view that they are likely to use the material in different ways, for example, share it with partners, or view whole scenarios rather than seek small erotic sections.

With respect to frequency, half of the 33% of Australian adults who looked at pornography were doing it once per week or less. The Porn Report states that '*Only nine per cent use more than five hours a week*', however, 9% of that group means that nearly 3% of Australian adults are using pornography more than five hours a week! Given that those adult users were primarily male, it means that about 2.5% of men were using pornography more than 5 hours per week. While this does not mean that all of those men had a problem, it means that a significant number of men are at risk of having a problem. In clinical groups of men the viewing hours are usually much higher than 5 hours per week (some men I see are using 5 hours per night!). However, it is not the number of hours but the impact on life which is the defining aspect of a problem.

According to the Porn Report, the most common media in Australia were videos and DVDs and, at the time the Porn Report was written, most of the material was bought through video shops and libraries etc. However, these trends are changing rapidly as the Internet becomes a way of life. Similarly, with the advent of smart phones, viewing pornography on mobile phones is becoming a rapidly escalating problem. This was not a feature of the Porn Report surveys because the technology was not available.

With respect to Internet usage at that time, 42% reported they were using the Internet, as opposed to 63% who used movies or magazines. These figures are also changing rapidly. While I don't have any research to support it, my clients indicate that magazines are rarely used now.

Only about 6% reported that they were paying for Internet pornography, while the vast majority were using free images. However, the porn industry is not a charity so the money must be coming from somewhere. The methods to engage paying customers are quite sophisticated. As I mentioned earlier, free sites often have poorer quality samples or short segments that end in the middle of the exciting bits to encourage men to go to pay sites. Some images cause the pay site home page to pop up – the frustration leads to an interest in better quality material. Big sites have cheap three day memberships which automatically go to monthly memberships. If you sign up for one site, you could find that you have joined three instead. The tactics are too many to note here, but my point is that you can still have a problem whether or not you are paying to view, particularly as most men do not report that they are using paid sites.

The complexity in the way in which figures are calculated can be misleading, but some authorities report that the average annual income of Internet pornography users in America is $75,000. At this stage, it makes sense that Internet pornography users have higher incomes. Men who are the most computer literate and have greater access to computer technology are likely to be earning a higher income. As the Internet becomes more commonplace (in countries like America and Australia, something like 75% of households now have regular access to the Internet) I suspect that the figures will level out. For the moment, it is sufficient to say that the assumptions about who has a problem are being challenged. It is not a problem of the poor – rich professional people have problems too.

The Porn Report also looked at religion and viewing practices. Basically, religious belief did not prevent pornography viewing in almost all of the religious denominations surveyed. Men, religious or not, from all walks of life were viewing pornography.

A final point to consider from the Porn Report highlighted a really interesting trend in relation to different age groups and exposure to pornography. For those born in the 1950s, only 36% of people said they had their first exposure before the age of fifteen. For those born in the 1970s, 58% had their first exposure before the age of fifteen. For those born in the 1990s, 79% had their first exposure before the age of sixteen. It is around the ages of fifteen and sixteen that the number has increased from one third to 79% of people first exposed to pornography at those ages. That is a massive change. Therefore, the younger reader of this book will have had a very different experience, and a much earlier exposure, than the older reader.

Older people are often not equipped to understand the world in which younger men have to function. There is no collective knowledge to share. Younger men have to face the issues alone and without understanding from others. Increasingly, younger women are finding that their sexual partners expect them to act like porn stars, leading them to resent the sexual acts of their partners.

Facts and Information

My main point in this section is that the viewing of pornography is common among men and that a reasonable number of men are watching a substantial amount of material. You are not alone. However, just because it may be a common behaviour it neither makes it right nor without problems. If it is creating problems in your life, then it needs to be addressed.

Key Points

- Viewing practices are changing but research in 2008 showed that 33% of Australian adults were viewing pornography on occasion. This translates into around 27% of men are viewing some pornography.

- Women were viewing pornography less frequently than men as 82% of the Australian adult viewers were male. Trends in research show an increasing number of women admitting to viewing pornography, although some believe that they may be doing it in different ways to men.

- Around 2.5% of adult men were viewing 5 or more hours of pornography per week. This represents a significant number of men.

- Internet pornography users had a higher than average income, indicating that it is potentially a problem across all spectrums of society and includes professional men.

Exercise 13 – Journal Reflections

- There are many interesting aspects to reflect upon in this section, but one which would be of benefit to your journey is to consider how your self-esteem has been impacted by your private behaviour. Does the knowledge that others are viewing pornography in high numbers help you to understand that you are not alone?

What is Pornography?

So what is pornography? It seems like a simple question until you look at it in practical ways. I have a quick exercise which will take a couple of minutes (see Exercise 13 below). I have adapted a range of levels originally developed by Max Taylor for classifying child pornography images. I have changed the terminology to suit general images. I want you to consider each of the levels from three perspectives. Firstly, in column one ("Porn"), ask yourself if you think this is pornography and give it a tick if you do. In column two ("Like it"), tick it if you predominantly look for these images. We will return to column three later. Please proceed to the questions before reading the discussion below.

While you are completing this section I recommend that you write your answers to the questions and record your feelings about the discussions as they occur throughout this section. There is a lot of understanding to be gained by contemplating this material.

Facts and Information 67

What is pornography? Is it photos of women in bikinis? Store catalogue photos of underwear? I mention these because if I talk to teenage boys, or adults reflecting on when they were teenage boys, the ones who became addicted to pornography in later life often masturbated to store catalogues or similar material. Their hormones were running wild and the images stimulated their thoughts. I saw one lad who had a collection of 3,000 women in bikinis. That was his sexual thing. So, although the images were legally acceptable material from advertising in magazines, it could be used in a pornographic way.

Another level of material is women dressed in lingerie or other clothing in various poses. This can be general poses through to close-up shots of the private bits (and similar material) or nude women in either whole form or body parts. Much of this has been the diet of mainstream pornography users for decades. Depending on the era which determined the closeness of the image part, much of this material was "soft porn". These images are designed to be erotic, but require imagination to activate the fantasy.

The parts of the body are significant, as almost all users of pornography seek certain body parts or body looks for arousal. Dennis Fredericks said *"every man has a preference when it comes to his attraction to women. Some men like legs, faces, breasts or any other body part. They prefer a certain colour of hair or particular ethnicity."* Legs, breasts, bottoms and genital areas all have many followers. A simple example is breast size – there are men attracted to large, very large, and small breasts. Although we talk of generalisations, the stereotypical porn model is a big breasted woman and that look is over-represented in the images produced. However, the porn industry is smart enough to collect images which fit niche fantasies as well as mainstream attraction. The many hours spent online is about picking your fantasy images. You stay online until you can find what you are looking for.

The next levels are to do with the sexual act. Close-up shots of couples making love, close-ups of body parts during sex, ejaculation ("cum-shot") images and so on, are material on which the majority of Internet addiction is focussed. At this level, the focus is now on a part of the act and is often associated with particular body types or looks. Viewers will seek just the right scene or action with just the right look. Part of the process is the seeking of just the right images and video makes that possible.

Now is the time to fill in column three. Put a tick in this column if you think that the behaviour is morally right. To anchor it into a perspective of relative morality, would you want your sister or daughter to be doing this with someone? Is it okay for you in the privacy of your own home to be doing these things?

The three highest levels can involve extreme fetishes and non-consensual sexual activity. The difference between the top three levels and the rest of the material is the moral issue. Look at the ticks on the page. Did you tick the top three levels? Most people do not tick levels 9 and 10 as morally right. Level 8 is more ambiguous for most people, but many will put it in the same category as levels 9 and 10. If you did tick the top three as right, then you may need to explore your beliefs with a professional. Many of these aspects are illegal and should not be seen as acceptable.

If you did not endorse anything in the third column, then you have a very strong sense of morality. If you could not endorse level one, there may be a problem. These are everyday pictures. If you endorsed 2 or 3 onward, you are likely to be religious or for some other reason have very conservative views.

The interesting question relates to the middle column. Did you endorse both of the columns as liking it and thinking that is right? If you like it and think it is okay, you do not have a moral dilemma or guilt about the behaviours. On the other hand, if you are doing it and do not think it is right, you have an internal conflict. You are likely to have some guilt about your actions. Excessive guilt about something can be crippling, but appropriate guilt acts as a moral consciousness. In later sections we will revisit this issue of guilt and beliefs. For the moment, it is sufficient to realise that guilt is a motivator to stop behaviour. Without guilt you are giving up because you "should", not because you feel you need to because of the act itself.

Significantly, if you have no guilt you are at risk of a serious violation of social and legal rules if you ticked levels 9 and 10. Rape, explicit sex scenes involving animals, and child pornography are all readily available on the Internet. You do not have to look too far to find an animal site, rape sites or other sorts of very heavy pornography. I am aware that many men are arrested and jailed in Australia for collecting these types of images. Some people are charged with possessing this material because they have an interest in it alone (a fetish), and some have other preferences but saved a few of these images amongst a collection of many others.

There is a different psychology behind someone who has an ingrained fetish and those who have some images in their collection of other material. The court may not see it that way, but be honest about what you are doing and get help if necessary. As I will revisit later, if you have anything that might be illegal, please get rid of it immediately.

For those who are viewing the highest level images and want to change, there are important sections about desensitising fantasies and fetishes later in the book. The techniques can be helpful in assisting you to change what you find arousing.

Going back to the question: what is pornography? What you ticked in the first column reflects your views but, ultimately, it is not what is being looking at which matters but how it is being used. You can have a shop catalogue and turn it into pornography by focussing on the sexual interest, or you could be collecting the hardest core images but not thinking of using them in a sexual way (as some clients with OCD may do). The issue of whether or not you have a problem is going to be defined by the problems it creates for you, not what you look at.

As you progress, this understanding can be a relevant factor because the low level material can be an important trigger which causes you to think about the higher levels of material you have seen in the past. A common relapse trigger when someone has been progressing is to see a low level picture in an unexpected place. I had a client who was triggered when opening an email for a holiday special. On clicking the email link to the travel website, he suddenly found himself looking at a bikini clad lady lying suggestively on a beach. It activated porn pathways which lead to viewing serious images. So much for his recovery process, as the relapse set him back again. Had he seen a palm tree and sandy beach, he may have ended up with a great holiday rather than massive internal turmoil.

Key Points
- The explicitness of images comes in many different degrees but ultimately pornography means that images are used in a manner which generates sexual arousal. It is not the image alone but the use of the image which determines whether or not it is pornographic.
- Some material is illegal. Get rid of it before you complicate your life further with criminal charges. If you are attracted to material which is at the higher levels you probably need professional assistance.
- Guilt about what you are viewing can be a powerful motivator to change, but it also generates shame, anxiety and depression.
- Too much guilt can be crippling. Not enough guilt makes change hard and could cause you to act carelessly.

Exercise 14 – What is Pornography?

Please read the section on *what is pornography* for directions on how to fill in these columns.

Level		Porn	Like it	Right
1	Indicative - Non-erotic / sexualised pictures, magazine pictures of women doing normal activities, e.g. bikini at beach, store catalogue underwear adverts.			
2	Nude - Naked or semi-naked in legitimate settings. Classic art, photos.			
3	Erotica - surreptitious photographs showing underwear / nakedness.			
4	Posing - deliberate posing suggesting sexual content.			
5	Erotic Posing - deliberate sexual posing which are revealing but not close-up.			
6	Explicit Erotic Posing - emphasis on genital area or implied sexual activities.			
7	Explicit Sexual Activity - explicit sexual activity during normal sexual activities, oral sex, vaginal penetration, and so on.			
8	Hard-core sexual focus - anal sex, group sex, and other hard-core sexual activity in non-violent ways.			
9	Gross Assault - penetrative assault involving violence, sadistic activity or torture.			
10	Bestiality / child - Sexual images of animals or children in adult sexual activities.			

4
The Brain and Other Factors

The Brain Pathways

What a marvellous device the human brain is. Even in this day and age of rapidly evolving technology, we don't yet have computers which can program themselves and change their own internal structures. Somebody has to install a new program into the computer to bring about the change and, once installed, the software generally works in a reliable and regular fashion. Our brains operate differently to a computer, as we can have dysfunctional patterns of thought but still exist in society.

Our brain is made up of a vast collection of nerve cells, called neurons, which fire on and off. When we think, the neurons are activated as a series of switches which fire and then recharge themselves. When we are born the brain consists of a tangled mass of neurons but, as thoughts and actions are repeated, neurons eventually group into pathways which become more well-defined over time. As a neural pathway is activated more and more, the neurons form clearly defined paths. The brain also has insulation (myelination) which forms around the neurons allowing messages to travel extremely quickly. The neural pathways consequently become neural highways.

As a student of psychology, I was fascinated by the early brain studies in which a small electrode was inserted into the brain and electricity fired into it to reliably induce a response, whether it was a leg moving, an eye flickering or some other motor aspect. Stimulating the particular neural pathways triggered a predictable, reliable response. The brain also has certain areas which are activated when arousal takes place. The medial forebrain circuit has been shown to be activated by sexual arousal. The significance of this is that there is a pleasure centre in the brain which is activated for a variety of pleasurable activities, including drug addiction and gambling. This implies that circuits that are made also include some hardwired components.

Another aspect of brain function which fascinates me is that there are biological predispositions to certain stimuli. Phobia research tells us that some things are easier than others to create a phobic response. For example, spiders, snakes, heights, and other dangerous environmental conditions are common phobias. However, many people who have a snake phobia have never seen a snake in real life, let alone had a dangerous experience with one. Accidental electric shocks are common, yet power point phobia is extremely rare. Therefore, it can be assumed that certain stimuli can result in stronger responses. The pathways for some behaviour are therefore easier to program than others.

Hold these general thoughts about pathways while I give you a few more concepts to consider. Whether you follow a religious point of view and believe that God put us upon the Earth and told us to multiply and replenish the Earth, or you believe in the evolutionary need to reproduce for survival of the species, we can agree that the human brain is designed to assist us in our need to reproduce. It therefore follows that we seek pleasurable experiences not only for the sake of pleasure (and sexual feelings are amongst the most pleasure feelings we can experience), but also for that fundamental survival of the species or, depending on your perspective, a God-given purpose to replenish the Earth.

As a species, humans would have disappeared a long time ago if the desire to reproduce was not strong and sexual responses were not triggered. It also follows that the differences between men's and women's reproductive processes can also impact upon the way in which they are likely to be triggered to sexual arousal. Women have cycles of fertility and there are times when they are fertile but do not want to reproduce. Offspring have the best chance of survival if a woman feels safe, secure and nurtured, because those offspring are very dependent and take a long time to reach a state of independence. Similarly, for the religious-minded, God has commanded that children be raised in families and that reproductive power is something that should only be applied in a marriage relationship. Both of these perspectives make a lot of sense for the survival and wellbeing of children. Underpinning this, it means that if the desire to mate occurs when those feelings (to be safe, secure and loved) are present, the situation is optimised. Therefore, for women, emotional triggers to sexual arousal have important adaptive functioning.

On the other hand, survival of the species, or multiplying and replenishing the Earth, will have the greatest chance for success if, in terms of male sexual desire, the desire is quite irresistible. Men are not biologically required to look after offspring, so sharing reproductive matter widely improves the survival of his genes. His desire is maximised if he can see and respond to attractive and healthy looking women (that is, visual arousal). Furthermore, if arousal was regulated easily it would limit the production of offspring, and therefore would be counter to the survival plan. This means that biologically men function differently to women on a sexual level, with visual arousal being a significant component.

Although not all psychologists would necessarily agree, I would argue that it makes perfect sense that women are more inclined to be emotionally stimulated and men visually stimulated. I would also argue that in the years to come, these differences will become clearer as brain studies become more effective in understanding which parts of the brain are activated during the sexual arousal of both men and women. These differences between men and women helps to explain why women have trouble relating to a man's need for visual triggers, and why men's triggers, on average, are likely to be different from women's.

This also helps us to understand why a pornography problem is so difficult to change. Eating, drinking and reproducing are basic biological urges. My theory is that Internet pornography has a way of stimulating and over-stimulating those parts of the male brain which are designed to serve a biological purpose, namely visual arousal. In the simplest terms, for many male brains the visual images of pornography are perfectly designed for stimulation.

Some research involving heterosexual and homosexual men who were shown pornographic images found that they had category-specific reactions. In other words, as expected, gay men liked male sexual images and heterosexual men were interested in female images. This also related to their subjective feelings of arousal (in other words, they felt aroused and physiological measures showed the same arousal). With women, the researchers found that women showed evidence of physiological arousal but the women did not necessarily know that they were being aroused by looking at images. In other words, men looked at porn and knew they were aroused; women looked at porn and had a reaction which they did not consciously identify. Consequently there are some interesting gender differences in hard-wired biology.

We can now bring the two main ideas of this section together. There is an interaction between the development of neural pathways and biological hardwiring for visual sexual arousal. The viewing creates pathways which are driven by a brain which is primed to remember the learning. The consequence of this is that it will make it increasingly difficult to give up the behaviour.

To explain this in more detail, there is neural activity every time you have a thought. Brain cells are activated and reactivated and gradually form pathways. While the brain studies within the area of Internet pornography are only just beginning, I am reasonably confident that over the next 10 years researchers will discover which parts of the brain are activated and exactly where those pathways lie. There is good reason to suspect that, while they may activate different parts of the brain, there will be a strong visual component within the emotional side of the brain (right hemisphere) in a normal left-handed male. We also expect that the pleasure circuits of the brain associated with various types of addiction will also be activated.

It may be easier for you to understand the process if it is likened to a drive through the wilderness. If you take a 4-wheel drive into a wilderness area and drive where there has never been a road before, you have to drive very slowly and carefully. On the return journey there are some tyre marks to follow and it is possible to go a little faster. If you drive down those tyre marks several times a day, it begins to form a track. As time passes, the frequency of driving on the track increases and a road begins to form. At some point the road is sealed (the neurons have myelination on the pathways) so the roadway becomes bigger and stronger and faster, allowing vehicles to travel faster. As soon as a driver enters the road it is familiar (nerves activate more quickly). Eventually the road becomes a 6-lane superhighway, where vehicles travel at rapid speed to their destination.

Similarly, pornographic pathways develop within your brain. At first you may have had to work to create them. Because of your biological hardwiring you did not have to work too hard to get started but, as the behaviour repeats, the pathways have reached the point where they are 6-lane superhighways. Once the urge hits the road, there is a very quick activation.

One of the compounding factors in this process is the frequency of driving down the road. You may think that sitting down for an evening's viewing is one trip down the road. Wrong. We know that the neurons will fire each time a stimulating image is presented. Therefore if you see 200 images in a night, then the pathway is activated 200 times (to be totally correct, with each new image there are millions of neurons activated repeatedly in bursts, so it would be more correct to say there are two hundred new bursts of activity).

Herein is the first important key in the struggle to overcome a pornography problem. The less you fire up the pathway, the weaker the pathway will become over time. The reverse is also true – the longer you fire up the pathway (view images on the Internet), the more entrenched the pathway becomes. Therefore, to get better you have to stop going down the road (or pathway) and, if you do go on the road, the quicker you can take an exit the better.

The second important point arising from this analogy is that if you do not drive down the road for a period of time, the road begins to fall into disrepair. However, once formed, a road does not go away. I would argue that someone who has had a longstanding pornography problem will have altered the pathways in their brain permanently, which is part of the reason why I believe that a cure is very difficult. Therefore, the factors that cause a compulsive behaviour to start with are not necessarily the same factors which maintain it. Why you drove on the road in the first place is one issue, but the fact that the road now exists and that you have continued to drive down that road, is a second and in some ways a more relevant problem.

If the road is not going to go away, what are your options? The option is to try and create other pathways. Positive thought patterns, positive sexuality patterns, and positive relationship patterns, need to exist so that they become a preferred pathway. Therefore, overcoming a problem is not simply concerned with eliminating the problem behaviour, it is about creating a positive and successful life in other spheres so that the brain functions better. The brain needs to have alternative pathway to use. In this book, when I talk about engaging in other activities (which can be anything from physical exercise to relationship skills), the importance of those activities is that they are building the alternative pathways.

A third important aspect arising from brain functioning is the fact that you are faced with a difficult decision which you need to make if you are going to master the problem. The problem stems from the fact that every time you drive on the highway you activate certain thoughts. Consequently, I am proposing an abstinence and avoidance model as opposed to a control model.

The addiction literature identifies two competing models. In the case of an alcoholic, one model is called controlled drinking and the other is an abstinence model. The abstinence model is best expressed through the Alcoholics Anonymous view that *"once an alcoholic always an alcoholic"* and that you are *"only one drink away from relapse"*. The controlled drinking model says that you unlearn bad habits by learning healthy habits. You must learn to manage your drinking without losing control. Therefore, the alcoholic has healthy drinking strategies, will space their drinks, set limits and so forth. Different models work for different people.

There are practitioners who argue that, when viewing pornography, a little masturbation is not a problem and in

The Brain and Other Factors 81

some cases can be helpful. However, as identified in the first section, the behaviour that you have been engaging in is causing significant issues in one or more of four very important spheres of your life. There will be major implications if the problem continues to recur. Therefore, you have to stop the behaviour from occurring. My argument is that if you commence driving on this 6-lane superhighway you will not be able to get off until the end of the cycle and by then you will have reinforced the behaviour because it has activated the pathways.

To put it in the simplest terms, you have a greater chance of getting over this problem if you avoid any entrance onto the highway. I believe that you are kidding yourself if you think that you can go for a short drive on the porn highway and come off again later.

However, as the Internet is an integral part of modern life, it is critical that you learn to control your non-pornographic Internet use. You need to be able to use a computer in a healthy fashion because you cannot avoid all computers. A later section in this book deals with time management. This section will help you to manage time, especially computer time, because most people with pornography problems have found that the computer has control of them.

In later sections I also discuss relapse. The highway analogy illustrates that many people successfully keep clear of the highway for months or years but, at a time of acute crisis, will recommence the behaviour. Unfortunately, they are not starting from scratch – creating a new dirt track – they are clearing the rubble off an existing road. Old patterns fire very quickly, and the road will soon be back in action.

This situation was brought home to me by somebody close to me who smoked cigarettes in their teens to early twenties and then gave up for around 7 years. In the context of a relationship break-up they commenced smoking again. Previously they had smoked about 25 cigarettes a day. Within 3 weeks of recommencing they were smoking nearly the same amount as they had done previously. However, they experienced head spins and hand tremors because they were overdosing on the nicotine. Their body was not used to those levels of smoking, but their neural pathways had been activated. The old pattern was being engaged while the body was not capable of dealing with the chemical overload. Sadly, heroin users and other drug addicts sometimes overdose after a period of abstinence; their body cannot cope with the doses of drugs used previously, but their brains expect them to be able to use those same doses. The moral to this story is that you are always at risk because the pathways do not disappear.

It is not a complete failure if you have had a period of time during which you gave up your pornography problem but life events, coupled with a trigger, caused you to fall back into your old problem. You are simply responding to brain wiring patterns. Recommit, refocus and then start to let the highway disintegrate again. The friend I mentioned earlier eventually gave up smoking and, as far as I know, has remained abstinent for over 20 years.

A concept related to neural pathways is that of the love maps or the mind map concept which John Money postulated in the early 1980s. The significance of this is that pathways for sexual attraction are laid down at quite an early age – five to eight years old (although I actually wonder whether it is a little older than this) – and it is thought that certain types of relationship pathways are laid down during critical times making the attraction ingrained. The influence of early stimulation on the brain is significant, but beyond the scope of this book other than to acknowledge that the brain is prone to various influences which impact upon the way in which pathways are formed.

The good news is that while the brain can form pathways of addiction and pathways of compulsion, it can also create new pathways. The building of new pathways, especially via techniques such as Cognitive Behaviour Therapy, has been found to be effective for these types of conditions. As will be explained later, a new pathway has to be built, often from scratch. The brain, like the rest of us, is basically lazy and likes to take the easiest path. Would you prefer to take a 6-lane superhighway or make new dirt track? Therefore you must persist with the techniques until new pathways are strongly established.

In concluding this section, brain wiring and neural pathways are only part of the mechanisms which lead to usage. Reinforcement and learning principles have important involvement in this process. In later sections we will discuss the role of behavioural factors in both use and relapse.

Key Points

- For many men, the brain is designed to be visually stimulated for sexual desire. In other words, the male brain is perfectly adapted to pornographic stimulation.

- The brain forms neural pathways which allow thoughts to travel rapidly. The more the pathways are exercised, the stronger the desire becomes.

- Repetitive pornographic exposure alters the brain, making it more desirous to seek images and therefore harder to stop.

- The less you activate the porn pathways, the greater the likelihood that you will be able to stop. It follows that, if you have had a significant problem, abstinence will have a better chance of working than attempting to control the pornographic image exposure.

- As the Internet is an integral part of modern life, it is critical that you learn to manage and control your non-pornographic Internet usage.

- The factors which cause a compulsive behaviour to start are not necessarily the same factors that maintain it. Ongoing viewing will maintain the pathways.

- The building of new pathways, especially via techniques such as Cognitive Behaviour Therapy, has been found to be effective for these types of conditions. A new pathway has to be built, often from scratch.

- The brain, like the rest of us, is basically lazy and likes to take the easiest path. Therefore you must persist with the techniques until the new pathways are strong.

Exercise 15 – Journal Reflections

- What did you realise about your neural pathways?
- How are you going to manage your pathways?
- Are you willing to commit to an abstinence model of treatment?

Two Sides to Every Brain

I grew up in the 1970s when women's liberation and equal opportunities for women were restructuring how society viewed women's roles. Much of this process has been very beneficial for women because it has allowed them to have more fulfilling lives and opportunities they previously hadn't had in westernised society. However, one of the interesting observations I made at the time was that there was a tendency for society to want to discount the differences between male and female functioning. It was argued that men and women were the same and should therefore be treated the same. Fortunately, in recent years there has been a resurgence of interest in the fundamental biological differences between male and female functioning. At risk of being politically incorrect I would like to offer some comments on possible biological causes to the differences between men and women.

In my opinion, the growing body of literature on the difference in male/female brain function explains, in part, the different experiences men and women have with pornography problems. Studies show that women do have physiological arousal to visual images, but generally speaking the percentage of women who seek arousal primarily through visually stimulation appears to be relatively small. Women typically enjoy emotional arousal, intimacy and closeness to trigger sexual arousal (as noted previously, women may be aroused by pornographic images but not necessarily consciously). As many as one in three visitors to porn sites may be women, but I would argue that many of them are looking at the material differently to men.

While there are a variety of psychological, societal and emotional factors, notwithstanding individual differences between people, I would argue that men are drawn to the visual stimulation. This visual stimulation is predominantly in the right side of the brain, which controls many factors but is under less conscious control and awareness. It is also emotional. Therefore, when that part of the brain is activated there is likely to be an emotional comfort as well as sexual arousal. In other words, visual sexual images can have an emotionally soothing impact.

The left side of the brain is predominantly verbal and logical. Therefore, when men focus on visual material, logic is low and emotional comfort or soothing feelings are at the higher level. This has important implications for the conscious control of behaviour. As soon as someone is in this state, logic becomes harder and harder to reach. There can be a trance-like state induced.

Patrick Cairns has written a lot in the area of pornography problems. In his book *Out of the Shadows* he describes this process beautifully – *"the Internet has an extraordinary capacity to induce a trance like state. People will spend hours on the Internet in which they lose track of time and reality. The addict's computer trance bypasses logic and they find themselves doing things they never imagined"*. While this true for a lot of Internet activities (such as gaming, online gambling, and use of chat sites), this trance-like experience is frequently spoken about by men who have pornography problems.

Underpinning a lot of the addictions is the desire for feelings of escape. For some people, drugs are an easy way of escaping. Escape is one of the common benefits reported by many addicts as it is what alcohol or drugs do best in their higher levels. They switch the brain off to allow a place to escape to where time is altered and the sense of reality changed, and it helps to make the addict feel good by mimicking brain chemicals. In my opinion, the brain enables this to happen for pornography users without the use of substances. In some cases, pornography users may add a substance which stimulates, such as amphetamines, when they go online. This maximises the escape. In my experience this is relatively rare, as the men I work with tend to use pornography instead of drugs. However, I have had a few clients who liked to binge on stimulant drugs while viewing pornography.

We have to be careful not to underestimate the potency of Internet pornography, because users frequently report that it induces a very powerful altered state of consciousness. It is akin to a drug for many of the users I treat.

Women seem to be able to activate and cross between the two halves of their brain more effectively than men. Therefore, women's brains are better suited to thinking and feeling simultaneously, whereas men's brains are best suited to doing one or the other. Many men become totally engrossed in the pornography behaviour, which becomes calming and soothing. They then seek more images to keep them in a semi-aroused state. Women, on the other hand, are able to flip between the two sides of the brain and therefore never become totally engrossed. Many women I talk to have trouble understanding why their husbands cannot stop their behaviour.

Many women also have trouble understanding how men can engage in looking at images. Most men I speak to find that when they are engrossed in the activity, there is something calming, soothing, or "escaping" associated with the place they go to. The nearest analogy for women is chocolate. Men *eat* chocolate. Women *crave* chocolate. Women seem to find something soothing and calming about chocolate that is irrelevant for most men. Likewise, looking at images in isolation of a relationship or intimacy does not seem to hold a woman's interest.

As I describe in the section on issues for women, because women do not have a similar experience, many wives and partners struggle to come to terms with the reason why their partner is looking at pornography and why they are unable to stop. Similarly, I would argue that female therapists need to be able to understand how the male experience may well be very different from their own.

To summarise, we are beginning to understand that male brains are different from women's brains and that looking at images has a soothing, calming and emotional outcome for men. But that is not all. Hormones and physiological reactions also serve a purpose, as many chemicals are released within the brain through this process. We will look at some of these brain chemicals in the next section.

Key Points

- There are two sides to the brain. In the typical right handed male the left side of the brain is verbal and logical while the right side is emotional and visual. Visual pornography seems stimulate the right side of the brain.

- Men who read stories (text) create images in their mind in the same way as men who look at images. The same process occurs with words as it does with images.

- Pornography seems to induce a trance-like state for many men. This includes altered time awareness and an altered sense of reality.

- Pornography is calming, soothing and escaping, much like the effects of drugs.

- Men, more than women, seem to get a complete escape via pornography.

- Women do not seem to experience the effects of pornography in the same way as men so they find it difficult to understand the behaviour of their partners.

Exercise 16 – Journal Reflections

- How much do you go into trance-like states?

- What can break you out of that trance-like state?

- What can you do to minimise that experience?

Chemical Cocktails, Sexual Release and Depression

Scientific interest in the chemical messengers within the body has been growing rapidly and I find it an absolutely fascinating area. There are a myriad of chemicals (neurotransmitters) and hormones that govern different functions of life. Everything from love feelings and sleep functioning, to depression and anxiety are activated by a mix of brain activity and the release of chemical messengers. In this section I provide an overview of some of the chemical hormones and then discuss depression and anxiety in more detail as they are directly relevant to your recovery.

Many of the substances I will discuss are chemicals that are currently being investigated so the science is incomplete (speculation rather than proof). Nonetheless, a brief overview will help you to understand the multiple levels of issues which have merged together to create your problems.

Of particular interest are the mechanisms of chemicals released during sexual arousal and sexual release, and those associated with addictive behaviours. These can have an influence upon our brain and bodies, and will impact on future behaviours. Similarly, there are chemical messengers involved with attraction, romance and attachment which have some relevance to the way in which you feel when online.

Let me briefly introduce you to some of these substances and explain how they are being activated during your Internet usage.

The first is the male hormone testosterone. Testosterone is one of the major hormones in men, however, women have some as well. Testosterone is a powerful hormone which increases sexual drive, however, some of its other effects include narrowing thinking and preventing fatigue. Therefore, at a physiological level, stimulating testosterone levels is going to trigger endurance. I am sure your mind is already making the connection with the reason why you can sustain long hours on the computer and that pornography seems to make you feel alert rather than tired. This is only part of the reason as testosterone is coupled with some other hormones (dopamine and adrenalin) which can also lead to very focussed, sustained attention. This also becomes very reinforcing due to the enjoyment experienced.

A second hormone is dopamine. Dopamine is one of the neurotransmitters commonly involved in many types of addiction. Dopamine triggers a variety of brain responses including those which involve movement, emotional response and the ability to experience pleasure and pain. Elevated levels of dopamine in the brain produce extremely focussed attention, as well as unwavering, goal-directed attention. Therefore, it allows for a focus on images at the expense of other things in life. There is an emerging body of research on the impact of using certain drugs to block dopamine in pornography users – the same drugs that are being used with heroin addicts and alcoholics. It is too early to say how effective this will be but in my opinion it may help to reduce the craving in those with problems at the more severe end of the spectrum. More research is required before I would advocate this type of treatment.

Endorphins are the body's natural morphine. Like morphine, some of the effects of endorphins are analgesic or pain-relieving. At high levels endorphins create a sense of euphoria and happiness. Endorphins are involved in helping to create a positive mood, so when endorphins are stimulated (as they are during sexual arousal) it helps to control stress and create a "high".

Oxytocin has been called a variety of things including a love hormone or the "tend and befriend" hormone. It is a hormone that we are only beginning to understand but it is associated with interpersonal relationships and healthy psychological functioning. It is a chemical which is released during intimacy and is sometimes also called the "cuddle" hormone. It improves trust, lowers fear and helps with attraction. Some interesting research has shown that, for people with autism, oxytocin helps them to feel a greater range of emotions. I have a theory that this hormone is released when men look at images. The images take on a special intimacy, rather than being simply pictures. I think the brain, via hormones like oxytocin, tricks the person into feeling more connected than reality would indicate.

In the chemical mix firing in your brain there are also the adrenal type hormones, particularly norepinephrine. This hormone produces feelings of exhilaration and increases memory recall and retention – it is both a hormone and a neurotransmitter. It is excreted by the adrenal gland and is often released to give the body sudden energy in times of stress. Norepinephrine, coupled with epinephrine/adrenalin, triggers a "fight or flight" response when released in times of stress. It has also been noted that a tidal wave of this drug is released after sexual climax. Therefore, it is likely that viewed images become locked in the memory more vividly.

The last chemical to mention at this point is serotonin. For a long time drug companies have been saying depression and other mood disorders like anxiety are caused by an imbalance of serotonin (or some related neurotransmitters). I agree that depression can have corresponding low levels of serotonin, but I do not necessarily agree that it is a cause of depression. To explain further, we were told in undergraduate psychology that there is a correlation between the number of bananas eaten in a country and the number of pregnancies. As a student I wracked my brain for the possible ways in which eating bananas could cause pregnancy, but the real answer is that the bananas are unrelated to pregnancy. In countries where there are more people, there are more bananas eaten and if there are more people there are more babies born. Therefore, these events are correlated but not causally related. Mood disorders certainly may have low serotonin levels, but it could be a correlation rather than a cause. A change in thinking can also change the levels of serotonin.

To return to the discussion on the impact of pornography on hormones, as I understand it, the research indicates that serotonin is released after sex and then the levels drop off. The fact that serotonin is released just after sex means that there is initially a natural anti-depressant effect, a pleasant feeling, but then as the levels drop off it may well trigger some depressive feelings at a later point. The implication is that serotonin serves as a natural anti-depressant; therefore engaging in problem behaviour at times of stress or unhappiness makes perfect sense. You are using pornography as a drug. For a further discussion of this topic, see Kastleman's book *The drug of the new millennium* (some of the ideas presented here are his).

The downside to using pornography to self-medicate for depression and anxiety is that it creates a vicious cycle of depression and pornography. As touched on earlier, if you have a sleep deficit caused by late nights, poor self-esteem, relationship issues and escalating life stress, you are a prime candidate for anxiety and depression. These conditions are exceedingly common in men seeking treatment for sexual dysfunction, with studies showing that as many as 90% of men reported symptoms consistent with an anxiety disorder and 70% reported symptoms of other mood disorders (including depression). The pornography becomes a way of trying to self-medicate for the stress, anxiety or depression, but it also makes the situation worse.

Professionals call it comorbidity when you have two or more psychological problems at the same time. It is important to ensure that you treat all of your problems, not just the pornography issue. If you have depression or anxiety, which is not treated, you are destined to fail giving up pornography. It is pretty easy to find a screening test for stress, depression and anxiety. Whether you go online, see your medical practitioner, or book a consultation with a psychologist, it is important to consider these other conditions and receive the appropriate treatment.

In my opinion, treating the comorbid conditions can help. The research into the degree antidepressants assist with pornography addiction is in its infancy. From clinical observation, early treatment of depression makes it considerably easier to address the other issues. However, unless you also get specific treatment for the pornography issues and create new options for life, then the antidepressants alone are not enough.

In speaking of getting treatment for anxiety and depression, I have until now only mentioned medication, however, this is not the only way to treat those conditions. Interestingly, many of the techniques in this book for treating pornography, such as CBT (Cognitive Behaviour Therapy), pleasurable activities and goal setting, are the same techniques used to treat depression. The question is whether you do-it-yourself or whether you seek professional assistance. If you have feelings of hopelessness and some suicidal thoughts I would strongly encourage you to seek the help of a mental health practitioner immediately. If after a screening test you have moderate or severe levels of depression, do not try to treat it alone – seek professional help. If you have mild depression, you have the option to self-treat or seek professional assistance.

In addition to anxiety and depression, other psychological or psychiatric conditions can be associated with uncontrolled pornography use. These, among many others, include Obsessive Compulsive Disorder (OCD), unresolved general trauma, unresolved sexual abuse experiences and personality disorders. The more complicated your life, the more you need to address the comorbid issues.

This summary of some of the associated chemical messengers shows that a variety of important chemicals are playing a remarkable role in causing, developing and maintaining your problem behaviour, especially if they are being released on a daily or near daily basis. These problems can be impacted by other types of psychological problems. This book primarily addresses the pornography issues, leaving you to address other mental health concerns or psychological baggage through appropriate means. I do, however, provide some suggestions and techniques to assist with those conditions.

Key Points

- A collection of powerful chemical cocktails are released during pornography use, especially if it is associated with sexual release. These chemicals increase alertness and focus attention, improve memory, dull pain, soothe and impact in many other ways.

- Depression and anxiety are commonly associated with pornography problems. In some studies over 90% of people with significant sexual problems have anxiety and over 70% have mood disorders of a depressive nature.

- If you have major depression or severe anxiety which is not treated you are destined to fail in giving up pornography. These conditions need to be addressed.

- Unless you also get specific treatment for the pornography problem, taking a tablet for depression or anxiety will not cure you. Depression or anxiety are not the only reasons for your pornography use. However, if you do not address these problems the pornography will be difficult to manage.

- If you have feelings of hopelessness and/or suicidal thoughts I would strongly encourage you to immediately seek the help of a mental health practitioner.

Exercise 17 – Mental Health Assessment

It is pretty easy to find a screening test for stress, depression and anxiety. Whether you go online, see your medical practitioner, read a book, or consult with a psychologist or psychiatrist, it is important to consider comorbid conditions and get treatment. As a starting point:–

- If you are feeling sad, depressed, irritable, of if you have sleeping problems and have lost interest in life, find a depression screening test. If these feelings are coupled with suicidal thoughts or severe depression, get professional help.
- If you feel emotionally aroused, have sweaty hands or a knot in your stomach, feel nervous, your mind is racing and you try to avoid situations or people, then you probably should look at anxiety screening tests.
- If you have to have things in order and if you become highly anxious or distressed if the order is changed then you should be screened for Obsessive Compulsive Disorder. This is particularly the case if you like to collect and organise things excessively and fear that bad things will happen if you do not keep the order or ritual.
- Anyone who has had a very difficult childhood, including parental violence, sexual abuse, or traumatic events such as death of a parent, could need therapy. The easiest way to determine whether you need help is to think about the past and, if you find that you become emotional, the issue is unresolved and help is required.
- There are other conditions to consider, but this is the starting point for considering your mental health.

5

What Causes the Problem?

Tunnel and the Funnel

One of the most useful ways to explain the experience of many men with a pornography problem is a model which was originally put forward by Dennis Fredericks in his book *Conquering Pornography: overcoming the addiction*. While I have adapted and modified this particular model to suit my understanding of the situation, I would like to clearly credit him as the source of this model.

The diagram below illustrates some important aspects of normal, healthy functioning in life and how that relates to sexual experiences in a healthy relationship.

The funnel part of the model represents the fact that we interact in a world where there is a wide variety of situations, issues, problems and fun experiences. In other words, we have a broad range of experiences in our life.

As we become intimate with someone, our experience of the world narrows down to a focus on them. The external stimuli are increasingly minimised. In other words, the wider world fades out as arousal increases.

The bottom of the funnel is the place which I call the tunnel. During a healthy sexual relationship, there is a point at which your focus becomes completely narrowed. In other words, just you and your partner are in the tunnel. Nothing else matters for a few minutes of time. This experience is relatively short and most of the time sexual climax represents the end of the tunnel. Occasionally, a major interruption reconnects you to the world. For example, if you are a parent you may be interrupted by a child walking in on your lovemaking and so you stop suddenly. Most of the time, there is a point of no return where the focus is only upon your partner.

As a result of the experience of intimacy and sharing, you come out of that experience feeling close to another person. You also feel less stressed and more worthwhile. You can then reconnect to the world and function to the stimuli around you, feeling better.

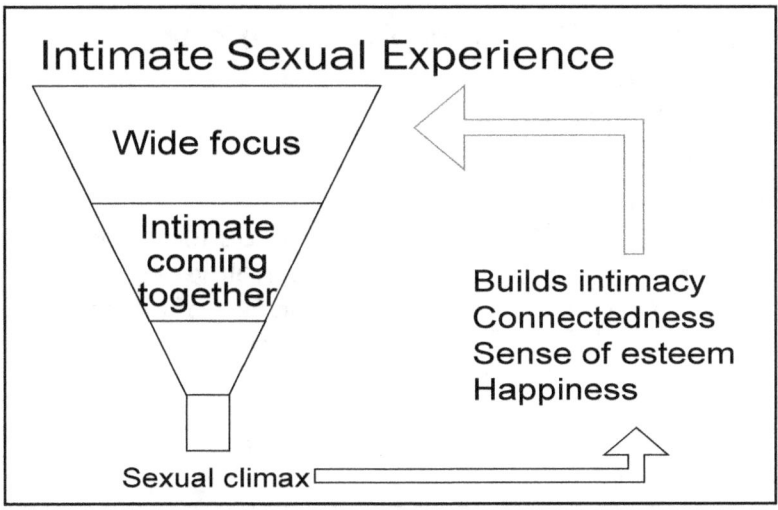

If you have a pornography problem the funnel still exists but, instead of a range of positive and enjoyable experiences, a large portion of your life in the outside world tends to have a component of shame, guilt, stress, sleep-deprivation or a vast array of day-to-day difficulties, perhaps mingled with some depression.

See the diagram below. Here the tunnel represents something quite different. The tunnel is the place to escape from cares and worries. The doorway to the tunnel is accessed via the funnel through the use of pornography. Scanning across websites seeking images, perhaps sorting and storing those images, is an escape to a different world. The opportunity to go to a safe and comfortable place, with a state of altered awareness, is the desired result. This time the goal is to maximise the length of the tunnel. This is done by maintaining a state of semi-sexual arousal and psychological focus. The rest of the world ceases to exist for as long as the tunnel is in focus.

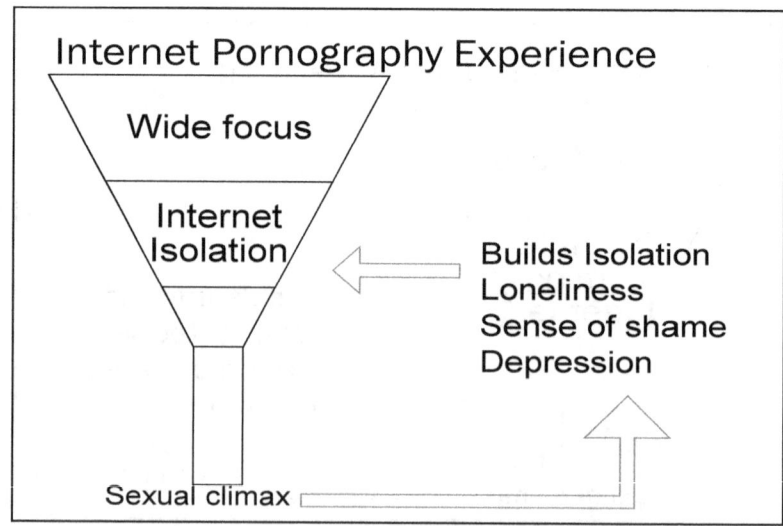

You may be able to stay in the tunnel for 3 or 4 hours at a time (some may do it for considerably longer). In my opinion there are two prime mechanisms. Some do it by using a sexual focus; others by collecting, sorting and editing. Either way, for a period of time, problems, guilt, shame and everything else has ceased to exist. As indicated earlier, the state is in some ways is quite similar to the effects of drugs or alcohol.

At some point you leave the tunnel, most commonly through masturbation and climax, but it can also be through sheer tiredness or distraction. Unfortunately, when you come out of the tunnel and back to awareness, the problems are still there, and the loneliness may have actually increased because of a lack of intimacy. For those of you who experience shame and guilt in the process, this will now be at its peak – so instead of reconnecting to a wide world, you reconnect at a much lower level. As such you need to cycle through the process again.

This process is also extremely self-conditioning. In psychology we talk about various learning techniques called classical and operant conditioning. They are discussed later, however, classical conditioning is where associations are paired together, and operant conditioning is where the consequence rewards a behaviour or feeling. Sexual release is an extremely powerful experience as it has both conditioning and reinforcing aspects. The images associated with the climax experience become increasingly arousing as our brains are programmed to remember things which are pleasurable and to avoid things which are painful.

Conditioning is also a method of shaping sexual attraction. The types of thoughts that occur just before ejaculation become conditioned through the powerful feelings which are associated together. If the thoughts are of an inappropriate nature then they become increasingly strong. For example, I may not find rubber outfits arousing. Having a powerful sexual experience with a partner dressed in rubber may cause my brain to seek the experience again. The rubber is now paired in my brain with a strong sexual experience. Eventually a point is reached when it might only be rubber that gets me aroused. This would then be called a fetish.

The key point from this is that you will seek images which are arousing. This makes the images more attractive so you seek further images. In the process you reinforce beliefs. If this was the only factor, the arousal source would become increasingly narrow. However, there is also a factor called habituation. If you do something over and over it loses the power it once had. In other words, it becomes boring to the brain. If you combine these two factors, it means that classes of images become more attractive while other images lose their power. This is why you might seek similar types of images but not the same ones. In a later section, I discuss how to use these experiences in a way that helps the brain.

When the tunnel experience is linked with memory networks it is easy to see why somebody who repeatedly visits the tunnel becomes more and more entrenched in that experience.

Key Points

- The funnel refers to the functioning of normal life as it leads to sexual fulfilment. Healthy functioning people return to the world from the funnel feeling an increased connection to their world. Someone with a pornography problem experiences the opposite. Guilt and shame result in a connection at a lower level.

- The process of online activity results in a narrowing of attention which leads to the "tunnel". The tunnel is a place of calmness and escape from the anxieties of the world. Once in the tunnel, it is very hard to exit. It is better to get out before pathways are reinforced and focus is narrowed to the point of no return.

- The practical reality is that the earlier in the funnel you make an exit, the greater the chance that you will be able to do so. Once in the tunnel, escape is very difficult.

- Images are reinforced by the arousal experience. Fetishes and attractions are altered through repeated pairs of stimuli with release.

Exercise 18 – Your Tunnel

The above discussion highlights some interesting dynamics. Draw your own funnel and tunnel to help determine what happens for you. Focus especially on the factors in your funnel, and the feelings or impacts when you come out of the tunnel.

Exercise 19 – Journal Reflections

For most men, understanding the tunnel is one of the most powerful things to do.

- What does this tell you about your behaviour?
- Can you see how you use the experience to escape feelings or problems which exist in real time?
- Can you think of ways you can use this information to alter your coping strategies?

Why That Image?

The images you are using will be particular to you but quite varied in comparison to other users. There is a small number of men who like to read stories while others like to look at pictures and videos. Some people collect the images and may have collections of 30,000 or more items. Others watch and then erase them. There are others who collect some images and then edit them using software programs to make them more appealing.

I have seen questionnaires which ask about different practices and behaviours. In my professional experience, I have found that it can be a mistake to ask too many questions. I had a client with whom I discussed a range of online practices. The client said that he did not engage in some of those practices during the previous week. When he returned the following week, he said that he had now engaged in that practice since he got the idea from me! My questions had triggered his interest leading to his exploration of it. Since that time I do not address methods or practices in detail, so I have not included a list of what people do so as to prevent this from happening to you.

My issue is not so much what you do. Instead I want you to take the time to analyse and understand the meaning of your behaviour. This aspect of understanding may require the assistance of a therapist but I see no reason why you should not be able to provide at least an initial analysis to begin to form some understanding of your behaviour.

Go to the exercise at the bottom of this section and gather the necessary data before continuing. This exercise is about analysing what you do and what arouses you. You will need to make a list of what you look at and what you are looking for – which particular images are the ones you find most arousing – and begin to look for patterns.

For example, a middle-aged businessman I once saw sought images of big-breasted brunette women as the target model for his arousal. It was not until his wife dropped him off at my office for a session that I realised the images he was looking at were effectively the same as his wife. In exploring the relationship in therapy, he was generally happily married, however, their sexual life was negligible. His pornography problem had started when his wife had taken medication for depression. She had been unpleasant to live with and had lost all sexual desire as a side-effect of the medication. Although she recovered from the depression, his behaviour was out of control and that in itself became a sexual issue. During the course of therapy, and as part of the therapeutic process, they addressed the dysfunction in their sexual relationship. The online pornography was effectively a substitute for his relationship with his wife, which explained why he chose images like hers.

Seems simple enough? As therapy progressed, the businessman also explored why he was attracted to his big-breasted wife. He discovered unmet emotional needs as a child, explored the symbolism of the breast, and explored his teenage attraction to a particularly well-endowed teacher he had had a crush on. Making sense of sexual attraction therefore has various levels of meaning.

What Causes the Problem? 109

A second example concerned a man in his twenties who was particularly interested in watching boys in early puberty having sexual encounters. It became evident that he was the same age as those boys when he was sexually abused, so at an unconscious level he was both acting out and exploring his sexuality through the images. Unfortunately, he was dealing with images which were quite illegal. Therapy to help resolve the sexual abuse also resulted in a change of attraction towards different images.

Another man in therapy with me had come from a violent and disrupted childhood. His particular interest in pornography was to watch black women being penetrated by over-endowed black men. He found the images were exciting but that they also caused him to feel inadequate. At the risk of becoming Freudian on you, he was trying to be the penis as compensation for his own sense of inadequacy. As with a number of men I have seen, he particularly liked images from the point of view (POV) of the ones having sex. He did not like to see anything of the man other than his penis. On one level his sexual fantasy was causing him to feel powerful against a background of very poor self-esteem, but on another level it was also contributing to his self-esteem problems by magnifying his inadequacy.

In a completely different sort of case, one man I worked with had a collection of over 30,000 images of all sorts of different situations. What he was doing was categorising and organising the images. He did not particularly care what the images were, and he had not looked at many of the movies he'd downloaded other than to look long enough to decide which category to put them in. This particular man was eventually diagnosed with Obsessive Compulsive Disorder (OCD) so for him the collecting, rather than the sexual arousal, was the important part of the process. There were also various other types of neatly organised collections in his life.

Not all men have a single pattern of interest, nor do all pornography problems have a deep psychological meaning. Variety in the types of different images is not uncommon. For some it is the actions rather than the type of model that is of interest. It is the emotional process rather than the model which is driving the purpose. However, if you can identify a cause or pattern to the types of people involved in the fantasies, it can be a very powerful source of information from which to gain insight into the dynamics.

For a very small number of you, drawing a connection between your behaviour and some unconscious psychological need spontaneously resolves the issue. However, for the vast majority it is only another factor which can assist you in your understanding and progress. The factors causing the problem and the factors which maintain the problem can be different.

Key Points

- A component of compulsive behaviour may be due to unresolved life issues, either current or from childhood. Resolving these issues can assist in the recovery progress.

- Not all people have a regular pattern, nor do they have underlying causes, to the type of pornography they view. For this group, the viewing of pornography is due to habit and training the brain pathways rather than any underlying causes.

- All people have a mix of factors which cause, maintain and enhance a pornography problem. The more information you can collect, the more options you have.

Exercise 20 – Defining Your Erotica

Make a list of the images you find most arousing. This should be what you look at online but may also include what you fantasise about offline.

When creating this list, go from general to specific. By this I mean list the context of the image (e.g. where it takes place); the people involved (e.g. for heterosexual arousal, what the woman is like, how she is built, hair colour etc.); and then progress to the scenes (e.g. what action is the really arousing component) using as much detail as possible.

Once you have this information, save it for use in other exercises, especially if there is a component of fantasy or images which are inappropriate (level 9 or 10).

For this current exercise, ask yourself if there are any patterns in the images you look at and whether it relates to your past or current life.

Exercise 21 – Follow that Feeling

When you have an urge to act out, or if you suspect that viewing pornography is serving an emotional purpose, take the time to notice and focus on it at a point when the feeling or urge is present. Just notice how it feels emotionally.

After noticing where the feeling is located in your body, and felt most strongly, ask yourself when you have felt like this before. When that comes to mind, notice what you are thinking about. Then repeat the question: when have you felt like this before? Keep doing it again and again until you track the feeling back up the network to its earliest component. If there is an unmet need, this will be the time when you discover it. This is an exercise which is especially relevant when there is a triggering emotion like anger or depression.

This technique works for a lot of people because the behaviour is often a symptom to escape the feeling. If the root of the feeling is discovered, then it can be dealt with. As long as you deal with a symptom, it will never change. However, just experiencing the feeling without judgement often causes it to lose its power.

Timeline and Patterns

In the preceding chapters I have provided a lot of information about some different mechanisms which take place. The purpose of this next section is to try and integrate some of this material to help you to understand the processes applicable to your psychological functioning.

I would like you to take a little while to cast your mind back over your development and make a timeline of your life. How to do this exercise is explained both here and at the end of this section.

Take one sheet of blank paper for each period of approximately 20 years of your life (at the end you may like to join the pages together so you can see your life at a glance). Draw a line along the middle of the paper and divide that line into units for each year. For example, if you are 44 years of age, draw the timeline across two pages. The first page will consist of your ages 0 – 22 and the second page will cover ages 23 – 44.

On the underside of the line write life events, unrelated to pornography, such when you left school, got your first job, first girlfriend, marriage, relationship break-up, car accident, or whatever has happened across your life in terms of major events. You can draw little arrows, pointing to the time the significant events occurred in your life. These should be both positive and negative times but not related to sexuality or pornography.

Across the top of the line you can insert your pornography pattern. Include as much detail as you can about when you first started, periods when you were not doing it, and then include the periods where the problem escalated. If possible, go back to any memories, the very earliest times where you were exposed to visually or sexually arousing stimulation, and indeed other forms of sexual stimulation.

Almost every man I see has a different profile of what has occurred across the bottom half of their line. Some men have very disrupted lives; others have quite normal lives comprised of mundane events. The more traumatic and disrupted the bottom half of the timeline, the greater the indicator that you should have a therapist to assist you.

The entries over the top of the line vary with each individual, but there are a few common patterns which I would like to discuss.

First of all, in normal psychological development the period of primary school years is typically called latency (around the ages 6 – 11). Sexual thoughts and urges do not feature, although in this society there is an increasing amount of graphic sexual material being presented and children are incidentally exposed. Unfortunately children are being exposed to sexual material earlier and earlier in life. Those from conservative and more middle-class backgrounds, and also those of religious backgrounds, often have later exposure than people of a working-class or welfare background, but nobody is exempt.

As puberty commences, which is usually between the ages of 11 and 15 years old, bodily changes and sexual urges become an important feature and sexual awareness becomes quite marked. Almost all men report sexual urges

What Causes the Problem?

and thoughts commencing in their early teen years. There is some debate in the psychological literature about how much exposure to pornography in those teen years shapes the sorts of sexual arousal and attraction patterns through later life. I hold the view that many sexual problems have their genesis in teenage years (if not in very early childhood).

It is completely normal for boys in this age range to be curious. Men in the over-40 age range had more limited exposure to material. However, those same men may have seen real people in a sexual way or naked (e.g. sisters, mothers, neighbours) and they may well have found their fathers' or friends' Playboy or other pornographic magazines.

The under 40s, and particularly those in their 20s and 30s, may have had a harder core experience and at an earlier age, due to the availability of the Internet and more liberal values on television which increased their exposure to sexual imagery. I am particularly concerned about boys in their early teens looking at extensive amounts of pornography on the Internet, and the consequent impact of that upon them. I believe they will be even harder to treat than those who were exposed to pornography at an older age. My theory is that the developing brain will be shaped and impacted to a much greater degree if the neural pathways are over-sexualised at a younger age.

A number of surveys are being conducted into adolescent viewing of pornography. Recent figures show that approximately 42% of 10 to 17 year olds surveyed said they had seen online pornography during the previous 12 months. Of those, 66% said they did not want to view the images and had not sought them out. Accidental exposure is certainly an important part of the situation. As a simple example, a family member's 8 year-old daughter had a friend of the same age sleep over for a night. The children were on the Internet looking at a 'Barbie' website. Their mother checked on them three times. In the morning, the mother decided to check the computer's usage history, only to discover that the girls had actually used Google to search for the word 'penis'. This is normal curiosity for 8 year-old girls but the material they had seen was shocking. The use of the word 'penis' had immediately taken them to graphic websites. All of this happened in a normal, safe environment. Therefore, it is very scary to think about the material that children can access, and in ways never seen before.

I suspect that most of you reading this book will have had your earliest exposure to pornography from the start of puberty into mid-teens. For many adolescent boys there is a spike in interest in pornographic material as a way to understand sexuality without having a sexual outlet. The only difference between boys from a Church and a non-Church family is the level of guilt experienced, and perhaps the amount of access available. The guilt may lead some boys to avoid pornography but for many the viewing of pornography just leads to guilt (for some it will cost them their religious future as they will leave the Church rather than give up their guilt-inducing pleasures). Curiosity is strong irrespective of religious factors.

Many youths will look at pornographic material and then move on in life. Some will continue to dabble throughout their lives, and others will become a casualty. I have seen 18 year olds with a 5 year history of regular viewing who are online for 20 or more hours per week.

What Causes the Problem? 117

The more common pattern observed in clinical practice is that many men move away from viewing pornography for a period of time. Typically, at a later point, something retriggers the desire to return to viewing Internet pornography. Therefore, a mixture of curiosity and exposure starts the problem behaviour which, because of all the powerful forces discussed earlier, gradually cycles to the point where the pornography controls the person.

What have you learnt about your early pattern? If your timeline identifies real sexual contact pre-puberty or during puberty, and as a young teen you had sexual contact of a confusing nature (for example, with someone 5 or more years older than you, or if you did not know what they were doing), then there may well be a fixation in the sexual attraction. This is especially true for some of the men who look at child pornography. Some viewers of child pornography have been sexually abused as children, and there can also be a curiosity pattern for those who had a same-sex contact at an early age. One of the key indicators of fixated sexual development is attraction to a very narrow range of stimuli, for example, with 8 to 10 year-old boys only. If you have a regressed pattern, it is important that you seek therapeutic help to assist in resolving those issues.

Whether you are someone who has continued to dabble in pornography from your teenage years, or have a pattern of 'underground' use which was later restarted by a trigger, the bottom line is that the process has some common elements. First, for some reason you were exposed to an image which your brain found arousing. There are a small number of people where it is a chance exposure, such as accidentally going to a website and then exploring it with curiosity; for others it is a conscious process. But, whatever the starting process, you tried it and a part of you liked it. Those of you from a religious background may have experienced guilt. As a child you may have also felt guilty when looking at forbidden material. This is the beginning of a splitting process where, on one level, viewing pornography was so intensely enjoyable you continued and found ways to override the guilt. For the more introverted, especially those of you with an anxious aspect to your personality, the emotional dynamics take hold very quickly.

This is where the tunnel and funnel aspects come into play. For a little while, with some visits, the escape into the tunnel felt good. You kept returning to the safety of the tunnel, however, the problems gradually began to escalate. Each time you visited, the neural pathways were activated and ingrained. The desire to visit became stronger, the frequency increased and, as indicated earlier, other problems occurred in life.

When you look along the timeline, look for periods during which you may have suffered from acute stress, depression or anxiety. For many men, pornography offers a way to relieve stress and to escape when life seems bleak and difficult. As indicated earlier, as the behaviour takes hold and sleep deprivation becomes a prominent feature, and as the desire and frequency increases, then depression, guilt and anxiety, and loss of self-esteem become a by-product of the behaviour. It becomes a downward spiral. One could call it a spiral of despair.

For those of you with an extroverted personality, or someone from a liberal background, looking at images fits with the arousal-seeking part of your personality – it was just pleasurable. Looking at forbidden things was arousing, and for an extravert it had a calming effect. This is also likely to habituate quickly so you will keep seeking harder core or more taboo images.

If you are someone who feels no guilt about looking at pornography and are quite happy doing it, it is likely that your problems were identified because your partner does not like the behaviour and it is interfering with your relationship, or a legal difficulty has arisen because of the nature of the things you have been looking at. The timeline might indicate that the behaviour has been consistent throughout the years, but it has only become a problem in a relationship. However, the situation has essentially the same aspect, in that there is a behaviour interfering with your quality of life. In some ways it is harder to give up because of the enjoyment and, at a fundamental level, there is no particular reason to give up other than for somebody else. The literature on smoking and drugs, for example, has for years indicated that the person who tries to quit for other people will find it a lot harder to do so than the person who wants to quit for themselves.

As you increasingly spend hours on the Internet viewing images, your brain is being programmed to certain stimulation. At first you may have looked at pictures of naked women, and then subsequently swapped to videos and hard-core videos. As indicated earlier, some of you will not have escalated your behaviour, but repeating those images over and over again is causing a particular part of the experience to play on your mind. The images have become a pleasurable escape from a difficult world. Aspects of the environment are signalling when the behaviour is to take place, so little triggers in the world are now causing your brain to think about the behaviour and so you repeat it over and over again. You have now shaped the things which you find attractive. The majority of you who view pornography on the Internet have a narrow range of images which you consider highly arousing (and therefore seek those images, putting you into the tunnel and the funnel) and those images then become increasingly important to you.

Finally, the timeline can indicate times during which you did not have a problem, or when the problem was a background factor. This is useful information as it helps you to see the types of things that were relevant to you dealing with life without resorting to pornography. The more you can make your life like that, the better it will be. Can you see things which you can put back into your life to make it more effective?

Key Points

- The pattern of pornography use over your life is dynamic and variable, and is influenced by external factors. It is important to consider which factors have been involved in making your usage patterns escalate or diminish.

- Puberty and early teens are times of curiosity about sexual matters. The material going into the brain at that time has a profound impact on brain pathways.

- Conservative backgrounds or religious influences cause many people to experience guilt over their behaviour, but powerful feelings ensure that those people go back to viewing images. To resolve the difference, splitting mechanisms are used to allow both feelings to be present at the same time.

- Those without guilt, or those who have high arousal seeking needs, are often drawn to images of greatest emotional impact. These may include images which are taboo or illegal.

- As you increasingly spend hours viewing images on the Internet, your brain is being programmed and shaped in accordance with what it finds attractive and arousing.

Exercise 22 – Timeline

Take one sheet of blank paper for each period of approximately 20 years of your life (join them together so that it is a timeline of your life at a glance). Draw a line along the middle of the paper (landscape position). Divide the line into units for each year. If you are over 30 years of age, draw the timeline across two pages. The first page will consist of the years 0 – 20, and the second page will consist of the years 20 – 40 (and, if you are older, the third page for the years 40 – 60). This will be the timeline. Then draw arrows which point to the significant events in your life.

The first items to include are general life events unrelated to sexuality or pornography. These can be positive or negative. Write them below the timeline. These will be events such as when you left school, got your first job, first girlfriend, marriage, relationship break-up, car accident, or whatever has happened across your life in terms of major events.

Across the top of the line you can insert your sexual development and pornography pattern. Include as much detail as you can about when you first started, periods when you were not doing it, and then include the periods where the problem escalated. If possible, recall the very earliest times where you were exposed to visually or sexually arousing stimulation, and indeed other forms of sexual stimulation.

Exercise 23 – Journal Activity

Review your timeline.

- What is your pattern?

- What does this show your about your trigger events?

- What does the pattern show you about the times when you either reduced your viewing, or stopped altogether?

The Two-part Problem

As you read this book, you will see that I am suggesting a model which consists of a two-part problem. The first part is that something caused you to become interested in pornography. The second part is that the behaviour, repeated over and over, has taken on its own meaning and place in your life. Your brain has been altered, you have become conditioned to certain images, and you have been on a downward spiral.

If you seek therapy, talking about the causes and why you commenced viewing pornography is helpful in gaining some understanding but it is generally not sufficient to help you to get better. For those of you who are regressed in your sexual development because of some traumatic experience or early developmental trauma, you will need assistance to resolve the regressed aspect of your personality. It will be necessary, but not sufficient, for you to understand the early behaviour. I say this because the bigger problem is that your brain and behaviour have been shaped and now respond to the problem.

To use a simple analogy, if you stand at the top of a hill with a small ball of snow and roll it down the hill, the ball will get bigger and bigger and bigger. The reason the ball started rolling has very little relevance to the size of the ball now careering down the hill. Analysing why it started to roll down the hill will not stop it at all. Therefore, the remaining exercises in this book are designed to help you get control, that is, to help you to stop the snowball.

If you look at the following stages you will see the level to which your problem has grown. In other words, you will see how big the snowball has become.

Think about your own viewing of pornography. Consider each of the following levels and determine how relevant they are to you:

1. Occasional viewing - At this level, in the mildest form, you may look two or three times in a year.

2. Growing curiosity - No compulsive thoughts but there is a desire to look and, possibly over a few months, an exploration of the Internet.

3. Emerging compulsions - You do not believe that you have a problem and for the most part you do not have one. However, the desire to look sometimes overwhelms the desire not to look. The frequency is possibly once or twice a day, and there is a little fantasy.

4. Battling compulsions - Here there has been a low-level battle for years. Interests have included some hard-core material. There has been some isolation and avoidance. You have been trying to stop but you keep coming back to it.

5. Impacting on life - The behaviour is now occurring two or three times a week. There begins to be some losses as it impacts on family, work and social life. Self-respect is impacted because excuses need to be made. The fight has been going for a long time.

6. It dominates life - There are very few days when pornography is not viewed. Significant amounts of time are spent either doing it or thinking about it.

You feel out of control. You have been covering up and lying about it frequently and the consequences are mounting.

7. Pornography has become your life - You are feeling completely out of control. The fantasies are occurring most of the time and at this level the line between fantasy and reality has become quite small. There may now be times when you are either thinking about or acting out those things you are viewing, whether it is with prostitutes, having affairs, or multiple changes of partners. There are now major impacts and losses in your life.

Other than for those of a religious persuasion, the first 3 levels are not yet a pornography problem, although level 3 is the edge of the slippery slope in which you are beginning to lose control. I would argue that if you have picked up a book like this, you are likely to be at levels 4 and above, which is indicative of a major pornography problem. Exercise 24 below explains how to use the numbers 1 to 7 (representing the above levels) on your timeline from Exercise 22.

Key Points

- You have a two-part problem. The first part is that something caused you to become interested in pornography. The second part is that the behaviour, repeated over and over, has taken on its own meaning and place in your life. Your brain has been altered, you have become conditioned to certain images, and you have been on a downward spiral.

- Understanding the cause of the problem is interesting, but you can only get better if you address what is maintaining it.

Exercise 24 – Timeline Variability of Use

On your timeline, enter the levels from 1 to 7 over the periods of your use of pornography. Look carefully at the times it has increased or decreased. Anything which caused it to increase should be noted as a trigger, while anything which decreased it provides useful information about what you need to do more.

Keeping Safe

I would ask that all of you who read this book to take a moment to review this section and, while reading it, ask yourself whether you have any images which are illegal or whether you engage in any behaviour which could be harmful. A later section in this book is for those of you who have engaged in illegal acts.

You have so far completed a number of activities to help you to identify whether you are engaging in behaviours which may cause you problems. If on the What is Pornography Exercise (Exercise 14) you reached levels 8, 9 or 10; or rated your use as 7 in the previous section (Two-Part Problem) you are engaging in behaviours which can potentially have serious ramifications in your life. Similarly, if you have included anything on your timeline which involves sexual activities with others on a casual basis, or is illegal, you are potentially risking your wellbeing.

Irrespective of whether or not you are ready to begin to overcome this problem, you have an immediate responsibility to protect yourself. If you are acting out behaviours with others, you are engaging in potentially risky practices, putting your sexual and physical health and any regular relationship at risk. It is important you cease. I have previously related the example of the young man who went to Bali to act out with a transsexual sex worker by having unprotected sex. He was very concerned about HIV risk. You need to wake up and immediately cease any activities that are wrong. In a later section there is an exercise on consequential thinking (Exercise 42). It is especially important that you consider the consequences of your actions.

There are also incidental ways in which you can be made party to an illegal event. A school teacher was sent a photograph of a girl in his year 8 class by SMS (this is now called "sexting"). She had exposed her breasts in the photograph. Although she sent it to him as part of a school girl crush, he did not delete it from his phone. He was subsequently charged with possession of child pornography, even though the girl had sent it to him! While on the subject of sexting, a 16 year-old boy received a nude photograph of his then 15 year-old girlfriend on his phone. He did not delete it. When he was 19 years old, it was found on his phone and he was subsequently charged for possessing child pornography.

If you have engaged in actions which are illegal in your society, whether it is child pornography or obscene material etc., you have an immediate responsibility to yourself to remove all images from your computer. However, simply deleting the material will not erase all traces. You may need to do some research or seek advice on how to scrub the hard drive of any recoverable material. Computers have browser memories, there are temporary files, sometimes there are backup copies of hard drives, as well as the files which you may know about.

In my experience, people can be arrested due to a variety of unexpected events. Some examples include: someone who had their computer serviced and the technician found material which was reported to the police; a child porn user's credit cards were traced overseas by the FBI, who subsequently provided the information to Australian authorities; a man was reported to the police by an embittered ex-wife; and another man who was arrested because his name was in the email directory of a convicted child abuser whose computer was searched.

As a Forensic Psychologist I often see men who have been charged with pornography offences and I've been employed to write a pre-sentence report. In the fantasy world they have created, they have a degree of conscious awareness of the risk but they kid themselves that they were not going to get caught and, more importantly, they spend so much time in the fantasy of their behaviour that they do not step outside to think about the risks. Please take a moment to consider whether you are taking risks.

In considering the types of material, anything involving excessive violence, children or animals may be illegal. One client was charged for having cartoon drawings of child sexual activity, and another client was charged with having stories (with no pictures or images) about sexual acts involving children. The laws in different states and countries vary but the definitions are often broad, using terms such as "offensive material" and "sexual material involving children".

If you have been acting out with real people it is critical that you take appropriate action to protect yourself. Make sure that any sexual contact involves practising safe sex. If possible avoid any sexual contact outside of a normal functioning relationship. I have had clients who have met others over the Internet and have subsequently been raped, assaulted, blackmailed or abused. I have seen people who have had sexually transmitted diseases. There is a very dark side to the world which is obscured by fantasy.

If you go to therapy, be aware that there are mandatory reporting laws in many countries and a therapist may have to report illegal sexual behaviour. Research this before seeking help. Sadly it may be the case that therapy creates more problems than it seeks to resolve. It may mean that you either have to be selective in what you share or use workbooks like this to address the problem. Having raised the caution, there is still quite a lot of ethical protection for most clients seeking therapy.

Please read the section on treating inappropriate fantasies carefully as there are techniques to help change an attraction from inappropriate sexual images to more appropriate images. However, the bottom line is that while you are fixing the problem you must immediately get your act together in terms of not creating further and bigger problems for yourself.

I know that for those of you with big collections amassed from years of collecting, letting go is very hard. I have seen some people with 30,000 or more images. It has been a life's work and they have been very upset to let it go. Remember the introductory sections on pornography as a friend? There may be grief involved with getting rid of a best friend.

Key Points

- You have a responsibility to yourself to immediately get rid of any material that is illegal. Cease any practices that put you at risk of harm.
- Do not kid yourself that it will not happen to you, because people are arrested and jailed for pornography offences. They are caught by all sorts of unexpected means.

- Ensure that the material is properly disposed of as computers have various means of storing data, and deletion does not necessarily permanently destroy the data.

- Some people grieve when they have to get rid of their collection. It has become a best friend.

Exercise 25 – Getting Safe

Immediately delete from all computers and disks any material which is illegal or potentially illegal. Ideally, as part of treatment and for your psychological and moral wellbeing, you should remove all material. However, removing illegal material is an essential initial priority for your legal safety and freedom.

Seek professional advice on how to completely remove the material from your computer. Depending upon your skill and knowledge, that advice could be via an Internet search or by contacting a professional. Be discreet about the information you provide to a technician as there may be implications.

Looking at Illegal Material

If you are one of the men who ticked the self-assessment questions related to looking at illegal images, or in reading the Keeping Safe section found some of your behaviour was putting you at risk, I have included this brief but important section for you.

As a society we have determined that certain types of pornography are acceptable and other types are not. Images which are "obscene" or "offensive" are often illegal. However, it is not always easy to define these terms because obscenity, like beauty, varies in the eye of the beholder. Generally speaking most western societies deem images related to sexual encounters with animals or children as illegal. While these two categories are usually illegal, it is harder to know what is obscene, but if you possess it you could be in trouble with the law.

As indicated in the section on keeping safe, you need to stop this behaviour or there will be serious implications. I believe that you need professional help if you are compelled to collect illegal images, but I would again caution you to be aware that many health professionals have mandatory reporting requirements in relation to illegal acts, particularly things which are sexual and illegal. Therefore, there is a difficult dilemma whereupon if you admit to looking at child pornography, or have a serious sexual fetish, there may be a requirement that the person from whom you have sought help has to report your actions. You need to find out your rights and restrictions in therapy to make sure that you get help while ensuring that you establish the appropriate boundaries to protect yourself legally.

What Causes the Problem? 133

There are a variety of legal problems associated with pornography. At a broad level, people can be involved in manufacture when filming illegal actions. This can include the professional manufacture of pornography, but someone who uses their mobile phone to film a naked child and then puts that on the Internet may also be charged under manufacture laws. Courts often deem the making of pornography a particularly serious category as it involves real children. A person may be involved in collecting images, distribution of images and exposing children to images, or trying to make contact with children for images. Therefore, it is important to know that a variety of things can be classed as manufacture and distribution of pornography. I am aware that men have been arrested for possessing collections of legally obtained material such as children in underwear. However, that can still be deemed to be "pornography". Similarly, the viewing of "young teens" can be quite problematic in that a police officer may determine that a person in an image appears to be under age, because the legislation does not always say that they have to be under age, just that they only need to appear to be under age. Consequently, you need to remove anything which has the appearance of someone below the legal age.

This is not designed to be a textbook on illegal acts, but some of the leading authors in the area of child pornography use (such as Taylor and Quayle) have been researching different usage patterns. For example, they have identified six groups of people who were jailed for child pornography offences. The first group used child pornographic images for sexual arousal. These may be people who have been sexually abused, but many of them have not been abused. However, their sexual interests involved children. Some only looked at child pornography images, while others may have had a history of acting out against children. There are plenty of offenders who view child pornography images and do not appear to escalate into acting out with real victims.

If you are the partner of someone who has been looking at child pornography, the psychological literature indicates that someone who has a conviction for past sex offences and looks at child pornography is at the highest risk of acting out against real children. If your partner has been looking at child pornography and has a history of some sort of criminal activity or violence, then they are more likely to re-offend in some other area of their life, although not necessarily against children. If your partner has a history of sexual attraction to images of children then they are likely to view more images. However, if I was a woman who had children in the house, and I found my husband had an interest in child pornography, especially pre-pubescent children, I would want professional advice from someone who is capable of providing a serious risk assessment, rather than trusting these general guidelines. This is merely provided as a starting point to indicate the risk.

Continuing with Taylor and Quayle, they identify that there are a variety of other patterns. There is a group of men who collect child pornography images as "collectables". Often they have very large collections which are sorted and divided. These men do not appear to be particularly interested in the pictures, just the collecting. As bizarre as it seems, some people collect stamps, other people collect pornographic images. There may be a comorbid condition such as Asperger's Syndrome or Obsessive Compulsive Disorder associated with some of these men.

There is a group of men who are socially inadequate, have difficulty relating to other people at an adult level, but share connections via the Internet. The child pornography is a "shared" hobby to generate a sense of friendship and a forum to trade images. Somebody of this nature needs some serious assistance in their social life.

There are also those who look at child pornography as a way to avoid real life. It creates an alternative world, a private place of escape from real life. This especially fits the tunnel and funnel model I described earlier. Likewise, as I have also touched on earlier, there is a group of men who habituate to images, and therefore seek more exciting images over time. In the process they seem to drift toward images of teen and then young teen images.

The literature also suggests that there is a group of men who seek images as a type of "therapy" to understand their own sexual abuse. What these men do not seem to realise is that at one level they may be trying to understand their own behaviour, but they are also in some ways aligning with the perpetrator and also causing the victimisation of children. They need to find alternative means of "therapy".

One of my colleagues, Tarmala Caple, analysed groups of Australian Internet offenders charged with pornography offences. She basically identified two types of factors, one associated with risk-taking and the other associated with sexual arousal. Whatever the pattern, the bottom line is that it is a sign that there is a serious problem and that you need help.

Writers in the sexual area would generally agree that any type of sexual pathology is a phenomenon which is very complex to determine, and has varied causes and cures. People who act in this way are not a heterogeneous group of individuals, but very diverse. Therefore, specialist individual help in this area is essential.

It is important that anyone who is acting out, or seeking to act out, against real children urgently seeks specialist help, notwithstanding the concerns about reporting. Sexually abusing a child is among one of the worst things that can be done to a child. What you do in your head is one thing – it is another thing altogether to directly damage the life of someone else through your actions. I would add that looking at images of children engaged in sexual activity indirectly damages children because you are supporting and providing a market for an industry which exploits and abuses children.

In addition to the professional help, following the exercises in this book can assist in the self-treatment of the problem.

Key Points

- Child pornography and sexual fetishes are complex phenomena with different variations. The more engrained the problem the more help you will need to address it.

- Some men report that they only look at pornography, while others both look and act out against real children. A history of offences against real children, or any other past offending, increases the risks of acting out.

- Anyone who is acting out, or fantasising about acting out against children, needs to urgently seek specialist help.

6

Cognitive and Behavioural Therapy

Functional Behavioural Assessment

Psychologists like to use fancy jargon. One of the few pieces of jargon I am using in this book is "Functional Behavioural Assessment". This means to analyse the patterns of your behaviour to see what is going on. To put it in a simple form, this is the ABC model. A stands for Antecedents (triggers); B stands for Behaviour (what you do); C is the Consequence (payoffs and costs associated with the behaviour). In its more advanced form we can also include the links in a chain of behaviour which can also be analysed in terms of the ABC.

Underpinning the functional assessment are Behavioural Therapy and Cognitive Behaviour Therapy. This relates to understanding, and then changing, the internal and external factors which are generating your pornography viewing. Using the earlier analogy, it is about managing the snowball

Cognitive and Behavioural Therapy

as it comes down the hill rather than working out why it started rolling in the first place. More importantly it is about mapping the highway and helping you develop detours and off-ramps.

The better the functional assessment, the more able you will be to specifically target the treatment. There are a number of exercises and activities in the following sections to assist with the process of managing the behaviour.

To begin with you need a good functional assessment. This involves you identifying A trigger (what starts you on the cycle), B behaviour (what you do), and C consequences (what happens afterwards which reinforces your future behaviour). These include both thoughts and feelings.

The exercise below (Exercise 26) summarises the instructions described in detail in the following paragraphs. Firstly, think about the last few times you have looked at Internet pornography. Now identify what triggered the behaviour. In other words, what caused you to think about pornography in the first place? Secondly, ask yourself questions such as; what did you do, when did you do it, how long did it last, what did you do to get the material? The consequences involve identifying what happened afterwards, both good and bad.

When thinking about triggers, look for obvious factors (I will discuss triggers in more detail later). Linking behaviour triggers with your functional assessment is the first step. The second level of the functional assessment is to analyse your thought processes. What were the thoughts you had at the beginning, what were you thinking (or, more commonly, not thinking) while you were doing it, and what were your thoughts and beliefs afterwards?

The initial functional behavioural analysis is going to be fairly vague at this stage because the process we have undertaken is clouded by a variety of different thoughts and triggers. As the behaviour has occurred frequently it is not always easy to identify the triggers. Using an earlier analogy, there are many on-ramps to the pornography superhighway. The greatest value in the functional assessment is as a refining tool. That is, as time goes on, each relapse can be re-analysed via this process – what triggered your behaviour, what did you do, and what happened afterwards? Each re-analysis provides a clearer and clearer picture of your problem, and the different strategies for intervention at each step. Using this information, you can get better.

At the end of each of the sections on the different components of the functional assessment there are exercises to help you apply what you have learnt to your problem behaviours. If you identify a particular problem, you can then apply a particular set of strategies to manage the problem.

As you begin to master the situation, this functional assessment will help you to learn from your mistakes. Analysing a relapse is the most powerful aspect of being able to get better. This is because initially there are numerous triggers, but as time passes you will be able to clarify what is driving the actual problem and what is causing you to visit the old friend rather than build a new life.

As described in more detail in the relapse section, a relapse does not have to involve acting on the behaviour. A relapse can include those times where the urge for the problem feels like it will overwhelm you. By analysing the triggers for the urge, rather than the actual behaviour, you will learn much about your behaviour.

The following sections discuss each of the three components of the functional analysis: the A Triggers, B Behaviour, and C Consequences. Following each heading are several short sections addressing different tools relevant to the process of your recovery. As there is some overlap between the different techniques, some tools may be applicable to more than one of the components

Key Points

- The analysis of your behaviour is essential for treatment. Functional Behavioural Assessment is concerned with the analysis of the Antecedents (triggers), the Behaviour, and the Consequences. Each of these elements can be targeted by specific strategies.

- The beauty of the ABC approach is that each relapse can be carefully analysed to ensure that you gain a further understanding of what happened. Learning from this process ensures eventual success.

- Relapses, which should be analysed, can include times when the undesired behaviour is repeated, but it can also include times when the urge (whether or not acted upon) is overwhelming.

Exercise 26 – Functional Behavioural Assessment

Functional assessment involves you identifying the A trigger (what starts you on the cycle), B behaviour (what you do), and C consequences (what happens afterwards to reinforce your future behaviour).

On a blank sheet of paper, draw three columns. Head one column "Trigger", the second "Behaviour", and the third "Consequences". Now think about the last time you engaged in the behaviour and list the triggers, the behaviour, and the consequences. Have a go using what you know now, but return to this again when you have read the relevant sections below.

A (Antecedents) – Triggers

Broadly speaking, there are two types of triggers: internal and external. Internal means that the source is within you, while an external trigger is where something in the environment starts the thoughts and feelings that enable you to engage in the behaviour.

In many respects the external triggers are the easiest to identify. Some of these are the conditioned stimuli which I discussed previously. What all external triggers have in common is that they activate the part of the brain which leads to the behaviour. Often, there may be a delay between a trigger and the behaviour – the process in between is where the urge becomes stronger and stronger.

The triggers are like the signposts to the highway. Once you start thinking about the highway it is very tempting to actually turn onto the highway. Once on the highway it is very hard to stop. Trigger management becomes critical for recovery because that is the best way of avoiding the highway. It is easier to avoid going onto the highway than it is to exit from it.

The following examples of common triggers should help you to identify your own triggers. Consider magazines in shops and service stations. A number of my clients have said that they were going along quite well until they stopped to fill up the car with fuel. While waiting to pay in the service station, they have noticed the cover of a soft porn magazine. At that point in time, their thoughts were minor. While they didn't have the urge to do anything, a thought process had begun. Later in the day, their thoughts gradually became stronger until, by evening, they bypassed their usual resolve and acted on their thoughts via the Internet.

If you identify a trigger of this nature then, next time you enter an area where there are likely to be magazines, you to need to prepare yourself (for example, by making a conscious effort to avoid looking, sending somebody else to pay, or finding a service station which does not have magazines). Even in this example, you can see how the functional assessment can provide you with strategies to help manage your behaviour.

A second common trigger, which is particularly difficult in warm weather, is fashion. Short dresses, bikini swimsuits, and other forms of dress create a visual stimulation which often leads thoughts down inappropriate paths. As explained earlier, in my opinion many men are biologically primed to be visually aroused. Unfortunately, we are unable to avoid going into public places and we cannot change trends in fashion. However, what we can do is choose how much we look and where we let our thoughts go.

Therefore, prepare to go out and make a conscious effort to avoid looking. This is particularly relevant if you go to beaches, gyms, nightclubs and other similar areas. In the initial part of your recovery, if these areas are triggers which have caused a previous relapse, avoid those areas as much as possible until you feel more confident in your own abilities. Avoidance, however, cannot ever be a long-term solution because we have to function in a real world.

Another type of trigger comes from conditioning responses. In the days of dial-up Internet connections, one of my male clients had a response triggered by turning on the computer and hearing the sound of logging on via the old dial-up connection. There are numerous personal triggers which become associated with the situation. The sight of the computer and certain websites may become reliable indicators. The brain has paired the trigger with the arousal which follows. Neutral stimuli, like a computer or the sound of logging on, should not of themselves be arousing but may have become paired to have a special meaning in the brain.

Sometimes people suggest that the pairing of neutral stimuli with an urge is a way of managing behaviour. For example, a churchgoer may be told to hum a hymn every time they have an urge. Similarly, associating a pop tune with an urge is associated with behaviour management. The idea is that it distracts you from the urge. If it works it is helpful, however, counter-conditioning often occurs, meaning that the hymn or song becomes a signal to trigger the urge. Imagine the poor man sitting in church when the hymn starts and suddenly he is flooded with the urge to look at porn.

Ultimately, if you face the trigger without the behaviour, then the conditioning weakens. It is not always easy to face the situation without the behaviour taking place. If you are in a weak frame of mind, and allow the trigger to cause you to respond, the pattern becomes entrenched. Consequently you should only do this when you are in a positive frame of mind and feeling in a relaxed state.

There are also special techniques which deliberately use these phenomena. Provided below is a deconditioning exercise to give you some ideas for applying these principles.

Key Points

- Trigger management becomes critical for recovery because that is the best way of avoiding the highway. Through your knowledge of triggers you need to eliminate as many direct influences from your life as possible.

- If visual triggers are a problem, prepare a plan to manage the triggers before you go out and make a conscious effort to avoid looking. By anticipating the triggers, you will have some scope in managing your problem.

- Neutral stimuli like the sight of a computer or sound of logging on should not be arousing, but they may have become paired in the brain to have their own special meaning. It is only by experiencing the trigger without the arousal that, over time, it will lose its powerful grip on you.

- Be careful about using every day common stimuli (such as songs) as a distraction because they can become a trigger for the behaviour. They might be common in the environment, so they could increase the times you experience the urge.

- It is important to desensitise triggers that might cause problems. If you are unable to deal with this yourself, most psychologists are trained in desensitisation techniques which can help eliminate the pull that some triggers have.

Exercise 27 – Environmental Trigger Planning

As you identify external triggers within the environment, consider whether you can make a plan for dealing with each trigger. Ultimately you have to be able to go out into the world, so the more situations which can be managed the better off you will be.

Exercise 28 – Focussed Breathing

If you want to de-condition a trigger, the first step is to learn focussed breathing. Focussed breathing, which goes by a variety of names including Autogenic training, has three steps.

Step 1 – We are all told that taking a few deep breaths can calm you down. What most people do not know is that the critical part is not to breathe deeply but to breathe out slowly. There is an elaborate biological explanation but what you need to know is that is slowly exhaling, preferably through your mouth, is optimal for a rapid relaxation. As you breathe out, try to allow your body to go a little limp. The controlled slow breathing allows for rapid relaxation.

Step 2 – The second step is to think of a key word to remind you of calmness. It can be a word such as relax, calm, chill, or anything else that works for you. Pair the key word with the exhalation of breath. As you breathe out slowly think your key word *"caaalm...caaalm"*. When you think of the key word, you are not thinking about the problem or anything else. The key word is a trigger for relaxing your feelings and it blocks negative thoughts.

Step 3 – Breathe from the heart. If you can shift your focus to your heart region, you can imagine the energy coming from your heart with each breath. This is to focus your attention away from your thoughts.

Step 4 – Frequently practice linking your breathing with the key word when you do not need to do so. It has to be well-practiced before it will make a difference in a real situation. A simple way to do this is to link this to a common activity. If you drive a car, stopping at red light is a common event (as is going to the toilet, or having a drink during the day). Each time you stop at a red light (or go to the toilet or have a drink), take three of the relaxing breaths paired with the key word.

When this has been practiced extremely well, you will be able to use this exercise in practical ways to help you.

Exercise 29 – Urge Surfing

When you have a well-established practice of focussed breathing, you are ready to use it as a therapy tool. It is time to go urge surfing! When a trigger arises from any source, the urge is strong. One part of breaking that urge is to ride with it, knowing that it will crest, then break, and finally wash away. Urge surfing has two primary parts: being mindful of the urge and accepting that it will pass; and breathing slowly and calmly to let it go. If necessary, you can also add some distraction at the end.

Step 1 – Acknowledge and be mindful that you are having an urge. In your mind say *"I am having an urge, I feel it my body"* (notice the different parts where you feel it). Stay focussed on accepting the urge for a few minutes.

Step 2 – Use your breathing exercise to lower the tension (Exercise 28). I recommend at least 12 breath cycles.

Step 3 – Say to yourself that the *"urge will pass"* as you breathe in. Focus on the key word *"calm"* as you breathe out.

Step 4 – Find something positive to do as a distraction (later exercises will assist you to prepare a reminder card to help you with this).

Step 5 – Later in the day, write in your journal how successfully you surfed the urge, and give yourself a pat on the back for your efforts.

Exercise 30 – Desensitisation of Triggers

It is important you try this only when you are feeling confident that you will not engage in the behaviour. If you feel that a relapse is imminent, it is not the time to try to desensitise the trigger. It is essential to do this activity when the urge is low. With this caution in mind, let us examine what can be done to reduce the impact of a particular trigger.

If you have a particular trigger, you need to change the pairing of trigger from pleasure to neutral or relaxed. These triggers are like the green lights for your behaviour. If, for example, as soon as you picture yourself sitting at the computer you begin to feel aroused and excited, you know you have a significant trigger to address.

There are two ways to address this problem, both of which will work. The first is in the real situation (e.g. sitting at the computer), while the other is in your mind (e.g. thinking about sitting at the computer). A good time to do it is after you have had a sexual release so you do not get aroused during the process.

In either the real situation, or in a quiet place (if you are doing this in your mind), do the focussed breathing exercise for around 12 breath cycles. Try not to think about anything other than the feelings in your body and the key word.

Now think about the trigger with enough detail to bring it into your mind. Notice where you feel it in your body (common areas include the stomach, chest, and tension in the neck). The urge and physical tensions should increase to a degree. Continue to think about the trigger while slow breathing. Try to breathe in such a way that the feelings begin to dissipate. Some people find that imagining the tension leaving their heart with each exhaled breath is effective. Gradually the feelings should subside.

Stop the exercise when your feelings are calm. Repeat the exercise on another day. Keep repeating this process until the situation no longer acts as a trigger. Sometimes this can take a few sessions, and sometimes it can take numerous sessions.

Internal Triggers

For many people, internal triggers are the more common driving force. Broadly speaking, they fall into two categories. One is an emotional trigger; the other is a sexual feeling resulting from basic drives.

Emotions such as anger, loneliness and depression, as well as anxiety and stress, are extremely common emotions for triggering problematic acting out of any sort. These emotions are the triggering factors associated with substance abuse, eating disorders, criminal behaviour, violence, and (of course it is no surprise) pornography problems.

Earlier we identified that for many men engaging in pornography induces a calm, safe state in which soothing and arousing hormones / chemicals are released. These feelings, coupled with psychological splitting and escape to the tunnel, take you away from the stress, anger, loneliness and depression. If you are affected by emotional triggers this is a very meaningful escape.

To cite one client's pattern of behaviour, when travelling away from home he would feel lonely and depressed, triggering the pornography urge. Initially when this was identified in therapy it was only one of many triggers, however, as therapy progressed the trigger was identified as the cause of a relapse following a significant period of control. In examining the factors, the pattern of depression also stemmed back to his adolescence. Viewing pornography removed his feelings of being lonely and unloved.

To manage the behaviour, he had tried to distract himself when away on trips. He would go to the casino and stay up late rather than engage in viewing pornography. While this worked as an alternative to the pornography, it also created other problems – wasting time and money, leading to a gambling addiction. Therefore, not only was the solution to manage the trigger, but there was also a need for some psychotherapeutic resolution of childhood wounds. He needed to learn appropriate emotional coping strategies.

Emotional triggers can lead to the behaviour because the feeling is present first. The above example is a case in point – feelings of depression leading to the need to escape. However, the situation can be the other way around. Someone may have an urge and then use the feelings to justify their actions. Anger is a particularly interesting triggering response, for example, where people allow feelings of anger within their relationship to act as an "excuse" to overcome internal barriers. A religious client of mine would have a stressful day at work and then subconsciously pick a fight with his wife when he got home. He would then make the excuse that *"nobody cares, therefore I will engage in this behaviour"*. It was a powerful way to override his moral defences because in his mind it was all her fault.

Somebody who is triggered by relationship anger is likely to need both assistance with assertiveness and quite possibly some relationship counselling to assist in dealing with the emotional triggers. There are books and courses which can also assist in the development of these skills.

With respect to anxiety and stress as triggering emotions, there are also very common reasons why people would like to escape from reality through engaging in viewing pornography. A client of mine had a severe anxiety disorder, was unable to leave the house, had no relationship, and was completely dysfunctional in many areas of his life. His pornography problem was a substitution for a relationship and an escape from a multitude of problems. This became a very well-ingrained pattern. To change the pattern an array of psychological interventions were required, both in terms of anxiety management strategies and the development of social skills. Some of these are beyond the scope of this book (anxiety management is a book in itself), although I have included some relevant information in later sections of the book.

The second set of internal triggers relate to sexual feelings. As indicated earlier, sexual urges are an important biological factor necessary for the survival of the species (or to fulfil the commandment to multiply and replenish the earth), and should be seen as a normal part of life. Later I will discuss the impact of pornography on sexual relationships, however, for the moment it is important to understand that healthy sexuality is a very necessary part of life and also essential for the management of pornography problems.

Sexual desire is the motor that drives human sexuality. However, the desire only generates a need for release. A complex set of thoughts, feelings and past learning determine how the feelings are released. Not all pornography users are driven by sexual desires (for example, those who collect without looking at the images other than to sort them), but for most men the urge is linked to pornography. It is important to note that the urge to view pornography is not driven by sexual desire alone. For example, someone who was satisfied with having sex two or three times a week before pornography became a problem, may subsequently be online 5 or 6 times a week, or even go online after having had sex earlier in the day.

At this stage it is important to consider aspects of your sexual life. If you do not have a sexual relationship, it is important to determine why there is a lack of what is a very normal part of life. Is it difficult for you to make relationships, or are there other circumstances (such as having a fly-in fly-out job where you are away for 4 weeks at a time)?

Similarly, are you in a relationship but the sexual aspect is not functioning? Unequal sexual drives are a common part of any relationship. No two people have the same sexual urges at the same time at all times. Therefore, one or both partners will vary in terms of their desires. How is the issue of differing desires resolved? Solving this problem is often the work of sex or couple therapists, who help partners express their sexual needs in a mature fashion.

To use another scenario as an example, a man who had been married for 30 years had a wife who had to undergo chemotherapy. Lacking a sexual outlet, and having a religious background, made it very difficult for him to have an appropriate sexual outlet. Pornography became a preferred option, even when his wife had finished the treatment and was willing to be sexually active. He had become so engrossed in viewing pornography that their sexual relationship never re-established. Initially his problem was due to her lack of availability, but once he started viewing pornography he no longer felt any sexual desire for her.

A more common situation for many clients is where somebody in a relationship has a partner who is generally sexually willing but on any given day or time may not be sexually active. For example, if a partner has offered to engage in a sexual activity in the morning, but for some reason it does not happen. The physical urge for sex is coupled with internal triggers associated with being angry and resentful, that is, the situation is used as a trigger to engage in the pornography problem. Relationship assertiveness (for a general discussion of feelings) and sexual assertiveness (to discuss intimate contact) are necessary to find healthy ways of dealing with the situation.

I would argue, however, that while the sexual need and sexual triggers are a common part of the problem, people who have a pornography problem do not only have a sexual issue. For example, if you want to achieve a sexual release how long does it really take? If it can be accomplished in 5 to 10 minutes, why are you online for 5 hours? As indicated in the funnel and tunnel discussion, much of the reinforcing aspect of the behaviour comes from the emotional escape, rather than the sexual release.

There are a number of miscellaneous triggers. One trigger, which is not uncommon, occurs in the lead-up to becoming sick with a virus when the body might activate hormonal systems to fight the illness. In the process, sexual arousal may be a part of the tension. Similarly, shift-workers and others with sleep disturbance sometimes find that excessive tiredness is a trigger because sexual release can aid sleeping. In the tired phase, the desire for release may increase the triggers for looking at pornography and therefore lower the capacity to resist temptation.

In a later section called the paradoxical key I explain some powerful strategies for managing sexual urges and restructuring thoughts using the very behaviour that causes the problem. The paradoxical key discusses the role of masturbation in dealing with pornography problems. Even if you are religious, it is important that you read that section. It comes a little later in the book because it is involved in several parts of the process, including dealing with conditioning and consequences.

> **Key Points**
> - Internal triggers are a common driver for problematic behaviour. Such triggers fall into two categories: triggers from emotional needs; and triggers associated with sexual feelings caused by unmet basic biological drives.
> - Emotions such as loneliness and depression, as well as anxiety and stress, are extremely common emotions for triggering problematic behaviour of any sort.
> - Anger and resentment are important emotions which are not just triggers for the behaviour but can also be used as excuses. The emotion anger has sufficient energy to override any well-intended desire to stop the behaviour.
> - Sexual urges are an important biological factor necessary for the survival of the species (or fulfilling the commandment to multiply and replenish the earth), and should be seen as a normal part of life. However, sexual feelings need to have an appropriate outlet.

- Sexual desire is the motor that drives human sexuality. However, the desire generates a need for release. A complex set of thoughts, feelings and past learning determine how the feelings are released.

- The critical aspect of emotional triggers is to have healthy ways of dealing with emotions.

- Sexual triggers need to be dealt with through appropriate sexual outlets. A healthy, functioning sexual relationship is an important part of a balanced life.

Exercise 31 – Journal on Sexuality

After reading this section, consider your sex life.

- What parts of your sex life are going well and what problems do you need to address to have a healthy sexual outlet?
- Begin to make a plan to have a healthy sexual outlet (later sections will help with this).

Thoughts

In the previous section when you conducted the ABC analysis I asked you to also look at the thoughts in which you have engaged. There is a very important reason for this. Ultimately, we are unable to directly control feelings because they are in the less conscious part of our brain. For example, try to make yourself feel sad. Can you generate the feeling of sadness?

Most people are not able to directly change their feelings. To demonstrate further, think of a time when something happened to you to make you feel sad. Try to remember it in as much detail as possible, for example, how did it happen and where were you at the time? Now I suspect that you are beginning to feel sad.

Hopefully this little example will have enabled you to see that feelings can be changed by thoughts. Think sad thoughts and sad feelings follow. Training the way you think (usually called Cognitive Behaviour Therapy) has been a well-documented and successful contribution to psychology, used for the treatment of many conditions. Managing thoughts is important because thoughts are a common on-ramp to the pornography highway. Triggers of many different types can initiate a thought, however, thoughts precede actions. Therefore, there are thoughts which lead to the behaviour and thoughts which challenge the behaviour.

Better thoughts lead to better feelings. Therefore, putting in place healthy thinking strategies is paramount to recovery. As a kid I used to watch Tom and Jerry cartoons in which there was bulldog character who would be tempted to do wrong. There would be a good angel dog and a bad angel dog – one on each of the bulldog's shoulders. Each dog told him to do different things; the good angel encouraged right behaviour, while the bad angel encouraged wrong behaviour. I have never met anybody trying to overcome a behaviour who does not entertain some internal dialogue, similar to the two angels, at some point in the process. Those of you with a religious background, or with a lot of guilt and shame, are going to have a huge internal argument about morality and shame and, therefore, you will have to work harder to override the voice. Everybody argues over the benefits and consequences of what they do.

A friend of mine explained the changing of thinking patterns along these lines: you cannot stop a bird landing on your head, but you can stop it building a nest. The way in which our brain works means that unconscious thoughts begin to affect our behaviour in milliseconds. Before we are even consciously aware, our brain is processing information. By the time the thought pops into our consciousness our brain has already commenced some action. Therefore, when a thought comes into our mind, there has already been some stimulation of the neuron pathways at an unconscious level. Once the thought is there, the choice we have is either to dwell on it, or not dwell on it. Likewise, in the earlier example of the Native American brave who wanted advice from the village elder, he was told that whichever dog he fed would determine which dog ultimately won the fight.

Knowing that thoughts exist is a helpful starting point. Before looking at your own individual thought patterns, there are some common thoughts typically engaged in by people to bypass their internal barriers to look at online pornography.

For example, these are a few of the beliefs I have heard from people in therapy for a pornography problem: *"It's no big deal, it's just fun"*; *"I'm only looking"*; *"Pornography provides safe sex, no disease"*; *"It's not like I'm having an affair with a real partner"*; *"I use it for education to make myself a better lover"*; *"It takes the pressure off my wife"*.

All of these statements make perfect sense to your brain if you say them often enough. On one level they are logical and justified. On a piece of paper list your thoughts in one column and then critically analyse them in a second column. As you do this you will discover a number of factors which make these beliefs faulty. See Exercise 32 for details, but in the meantime look at each of the thoughts again:

Thought	Challenge
"It's no big deal, it's just for fun".	Well, if it's just for fun, why did you buy this book? Why are you staying up for 2 to 3 hours a night? Why has the behaviour got control of you?
"I'm only looking".	You may "only" be looking, except you are activating pathways in the brain. If you have moral concerns, there are a range of issues relating to the number of pornographic models who have been exploited, sexually abused, or who have no real choice about being in the industry.
"Pornography provides safe sex, no disease".	It is correct that it avoids diseases, but all of the points for the first belief apply here. It is creating problems in your life and therefore it no longer serves the purpose of safe sex.

Thought	Challenge
"It's not like I'm having an affair with a real partner".	It is true that you are not committing a sexual act with another partner, but many women feel that their partner is committing emotional infidelity, if not sexual infidelity. They feel cheated out of the relationship. The most significant problem with this is that instead of building intimacy in the relationship most important to you, you are building isolation from the relationship.
"It takes the pressure off my wife".	Yes, that may well be a justification, but are her sexual needs being met? Is your relationship growing and progressing? Do you have appropriate intimacy?
"I use it for education to make me a better lover"	There is a fundamental flaw to the logic in this statement, in that repetitive viewing of pornography tends to objectify women and creates a false illusion about what women want sexually. Although it expands a repertoire of behaviour, it is based on an artificial and staged view of sexuality and generally increases people's sense of sexual inadequacy. If you want sexual education, do not view pornography – obtain one of the very good sex education books which are readily available.

When analysing your beliefs it is critical to understand that they can be subtle and powerful. Thoughts enable you to bypass your normal conscience and slip into a state which is akin to having a split brain.

I would also like to point out that while thoughts can lead to feelings, in this area the battle often runs along two hemispheres of the brain. The urge appears to exist in the less conscious part of the brain while the thoughts exist in the conscious part. You need to battle to maintain control in the logical part of the brain. For many men, as they go into the tunnel, thoughts narrow to the point where they do not allow logic to enter. When in this state it is almost impossible to bring logic into place. Therefore, while in the funnel, thought techniques can be useful. Once in the tunnel it is often too late to do much about it, although even within the tunnel the narrowness of it can fluctuate. On the upswing of a fluctuation there is sometimes enough scope to escape. One of the most exciting moments during someone's recovery is when they actually pull themselves out of the tunnel during an episode.

There are several basic thought control techniques which are really useful. The first of those has already been discussed. You identify the negative thought, and then you challenge the belief. By focussing on the belief you motivate yourself away, rather than to, the behaviour.

A second type of thought control involves a technique called "Thought Stopping" (Exercise 33 below). When a thought pops into your mind, it is critical that you think – or if you are by yourself, say – the word "*Stop*" (to fine tune the process, say "stop" when breathing in). As arousal increases, take a big breath, breathe out slowly, and replace the thought with the key word (from Exercise 26). In this process you remind yourself to stop thinking. The breathing out slowly helps your body to calm itself, and replacing the negative thought with a positive key word allows for a replacement thought.

A more advanced type of thought control uses distraction techniques. These techniques simply require you distract yourself (Exercise 35). Try an experiment to see if you can delay the urge that arises. To begin with you might only delay the urge for a few moments. Even though you might still react, you will have exercised some control over the behaviour pattern. As you practise distraction to delay the urge you will have more successes until you will eventually become so absorbed in the alternative activity that the urge dissipates completely. To begin with, you might like to try delaying only mild or moderate urges.

I would readily agree that when the urge is screaming at you, something as simple as thought stopping will struggle to make a difference. This is where it is important for you develop an escape plan (Exercise 34). If you are in a situation where the urge has become extremely high, a pre-set plan of action can be put into place. Activities such as ringing a friend, getting out of the house, or going for a walk around the block will help stop the negative thinking. Coupled with thought stopping, having a rational, logical plan, as well as challenging the beliefs, maximises the chance that the urge will pass.

Key Points

- I have never met anybody trying to overcome a behaviour who does not entertain some internal dialogue. Everybody will argue over the benefits and consequences of what they do, and listening to those arguments can help.

- Once the thought is there, the choice we have is to dwell on it, or not dwell on it.

- You cannot stop a bird landing on your head, but you can stop it building a nest.

- For many men, as they go into the tunnel, thoughts narrow to the point where they do not allow logic to consciously enter. Once in this state it is almost impossible to bring logic into place. Therefore stop the thoughts early.

Exercise 32 – Challenging Thoughts

On a piece of paper, draw two columns. Make a list of the thoughts that you use to rationalise your way past your internal barriers, or to justify engaging in the behaviour.

In the second column challenge each thought with a logical statement. If you are unable to challenge the thought, consider whether you need some professional help to deal with it, or if the thought is actually real. For example, if you wrote "*I want sex but my wife is away for three weeks*" it is a real statement. However, to challenge that statement ask yourself why you need pornography to deal with the urge.

Exercise 33 – Thought Stopping

A useful thought control technique is called *"Thought Stopping"*. When a thought pops into your mind, it is critical that you think (or if alone, say out loud) the word "Stop". Coupled with the exercise on breathing (Exercise 26), thought stopping can be very effective.

Exercise 34 – Escape Plan

An escape plan is a pre-planned action sequence available for you to implement when all else is not working. It is best to list the plan on a card and carry it in your wallet, or have it typed into your phone or iPad. The plan tells you what to do when the urge is becoming too strong for you to cope with.

You might like to write ten actions on a card and do them all before allowing yourself to action the urge (some of these actions might include phoning a friend, doing ten push-ups, walking around the block, reading a section of this book, reviewing your list of consequences, writing your feelings in your journal, and asking yourself where else you have felt like that before (Exercise 21)).

Sometimes masturbation is a useful action to have on the list. For a church goer it might be the action of last resort (it is better to release sexual tension than to look at pornography, even though the sexual release may happen eventually anyway), while for others it might be one of the first actions (to cause an early release without the thoughts (see the section on paradoxical keys).

In a perfect world, you might get the urge and then use the plan to stop the behaviour. However, try the plan because relapse is common in the early stages. In any case, if the actions work well keep them on the list. You should remove and replace those actions that do not work.

Exercise 35 – Distraction techniques

Identify and learn those activities which are most effective in absorbing your mind and distracting you. When you are neither stressed nor feeling an urge to view pornography, practise using these activities. As soon as you have a few options that work, you can begin to use them to delay acting when you feel the urge. Some example techniques are included in the following paragraphs.

The card game solitaire or patience has been effective for many clients. It is accessible – you can carry a pack of cards with you – and it does not take long to set up. It is physical and involves the body and mind. It is also a little addictive because you want to continue playing until you complete the game successfully. Once started it does not demand much effort and clients have reported that it helps to switch off the mind.

Calling a friend and talking for a while is also quite effective for some people. When you focus on someone else it is easier to forget about your own issues. It is distracting to listen to, and interact with, a friend. You may decide to discuss your true feelings with a close friend, or you might have a more superficial conversation if you don't wish to focus on your feelings.

Playing with a favourite pet can also be used to change your mood and distract you from feelings which you cannot as yet control.

Sometimes instrumental activities, such as cleaning or gardening, can be effective at providing you with some timeout when you are feeling overwhelmed.

Behaviour

The B in the ABC relates to behaviour. This is what you do when the problem occurs. The more you understand what you are doing, when you do it, and how you do it, the better your management strategies will be. It is also important to consider what else you might have done if you had not engaged in the behaviour. The time taken to sit in front of a computer, are hours of your life in which no other things are done. It has also been said that time has no shelf life. If you do not use it today, you cannot use it tomorrow. Therefore you are wasting a non-renewable asset.

The analysis of the behaviour happens on multiple levels – the micro level of the how, where and what you do during the session, and the macro level of how your life is structured and the patterns you have created for the pornography problem to occur.

There are several components to the behavioural aspect of treatment, but the key aspect is based on the highway philosophy explained earlier. Each time you succeed in avoiding the pornography pathways in your brain, you gradually regain control. It is preferable to stay off the highway so that there is no neural activation and reinforcement of the brain pathways. Alternatively you need to find the off-ramps quickly so that you are on the highway for only a short period of time. If you activate the neural pathways you will not get better, but if you keep off the highway it will gradually break down.

As well as avoiding pathway activation, it is important to consider your life from the perspective that simply stopping the behaviour will leave a deficit in your life. Remember the section where I discussed why the problem is also your friend? Well, you need to develop some new friends in your life. One of the first friends I suggest you become re-acquainted with is exercise. Most people living a cyberlife lack exercise. As soon as you start engaging in physical exercise, you will find that it helps to stimulate various positive aspects in the brain, helps you to feel better about yourself, and is a most useful way of dissipating both stress chemicals and emotions.

Regular physical exercise has tremendous physical benefits, which is the reason why doctors recommend it for good health. However, research on the role of exercise in mental health is also extremely encouraging. Currently, one of the most effective known strategies for depression (outside of medication or psychotherapy) is exercise. Given that the common triggers for you are emotional, and also that there is a high probability that you have a mood disorder (stress, depression or anxiety), then what are you waiting for? Incorporate some exercise into your life.

A funny incident occurred during therapy when I recommended to a strongly religious man, who was in a very poor marriage, to use his exercise bike to deal with urges. Masturbation was not an option for him, and his conservative wife was so appalled by his use of pornography that she refused any sexual contact. I suggested that he try to deal with his urges by riding his exercise bike. He came back a week later, glowing with success because he'd not used pornography or masturbated, but said he'd had over 20 hours of bike riding during the week! The moral of the story is that replacing the problem has to be more than substituting one issue for another. An especially good example of this, described earlier, was the man who used gambling to escape the pornography. In the case of the man who used his exercise bike, it was the lesser of two evils and a good starting point, however, it would not be a sustainable long-term solution.

A new "friend" needs to be in the form of some sort of interest or activity. Those of you who have identified loneliness as an issue need to find some social activities in which to engage. Activities earlier in this book helped you to review what you have done in your life. Now go to the exercises below and put together a structured idea of what you would like to do to create a new pattern of behaviour.

When somebody like you has created an intense cyberlife you need to reconnect with the real world. In my experience, most people with pornography problems have gradually cut out all of the positive activities from their life, including their social activities, sporting activities, and club memberships. They no longer do anything other than use the Internet. It is important that you start to find another passion to help redirect aspects of your life. If you want to feel good about yourself you need to have a healthy functioning social life.

In the following sections I discuss two other important aspects of behaviour. The first of those is restricting the risks in your environment. From examining and learning from the way the behaviour occurs, there are simple practical things that can be changed. A simple example is, if you do not have a computer at home you cannot look at online pornography at home. Unfortunately, life is not that simple and computers are a part of life. The section on Practical Strategies offers some simple environmental solutions to assist in managing the problem.

Another behavioural aspect that requires examination is time management. Studies show that as many as 96% of people with pornography problems rate time management as one of their biggest issues. The section called Time Management includes a series of exercises to assist you to manage your time more effectively.

> **Key Points**
>
> - The analysis of the behaviour happens at multiple levels. There is the micro level of the how, where and what you do in the individual session. There are the macro aspects of how your life has created the structure for the pornography problem to occur.
>
> - Behavioural management is based on the highway philosophy. Build a pattern of behaviour so that it maximises your chances of avoiding the pornography pathways. Build exits and escape routes to get off the old highway. Then build a new highway.
>
> - Most people living a cyberlife lack exercise. Physical exercise stimulates various positive aspects in the brain, helps improve self-esteem, and dissipates both stress chemicals and emotions.
>
> - It is essential to reconnect with the real world. Rebuild positive activities such as, social activities, sporting activities, and club memberships. A productive life needs to be rebuilt.

Exercise 36 – Journal Reflections

You reviewed your behaviour in the section on Functional Behavioural Analysis. After reading the above section about the behaviour, note in your journal those things which need to change, and add to the ABC model anything that may need to be addressed.

Exercise 37 – Becoming Physical

Physical exercise is very helpful for good mental processing and physical health. It is also a useful way of dissipating urges. Therefore regular exercise (for general health) and short bursts of vigorous exercise are essential for managing urges. Feeling physically healthy is also good for your self-esteem. Get some exercise.

When starting an exercise routine, common sense is important. If there is any reason to doubt your physical condition, such as being overweight, heart problems, or being over 40 years of age, please ensure that you get a medical check-up before you start. If your fitness level is poor, start gently and build up. Seek advice from a certified sports trainer to build your level of fitness.

Exercise 38 – Finding New "Friends"

On a blank sheet of paper, draw a line down the middle and write *"Before"* in first column and *"Future"* in the other column. In the *"Before"* column, try to recollect all of the activities you used to do and enjoy, such as sporting activities, going out, socialising with friends, horse riding, fishing, or whatever else you may have done.

Cognitive and Behavioural Therapy

In the *"Future"* column write down any activity which you would like to take on, whether it is an overseas trip, a new sporting activity, a university course, or whatever else you desire. Now circle all of those which you think are possible to integrate into your life reasonably quickly. Put an asterisk against something which you can do within the next 72 hours (that could be something as simple as going for a walk, or signing up for a course or class). Take your planner and note when you are going to start that activity.

Now review the list again and pick some items which you would like to accomplish in the longer term. Some things will take time to organise (for example an overseas trip or a university course may require substantial organisation), but if that is your goal identify the steps necessary to achieve it. By including both short and long term activities, you can begin to build the life which you either had before or would like to have now. There are some activities that people grow out of or that might no longer be possible, for example, an injury that prevents sporting activity. The important thing is that you commence your new or re-established activities now. It is time to turn off the computer and do something in the real world.

When you read these suggestions, if you think that you do not have the time, then you may need some professional assistance to rebuild your life in a functional manner.

Practical Strategies

A necessary step to reclaiming your life is to clean out everything that is likely to trigger some thought or reaction leading to pornography, or which can be used to make the problem happen. As Oscar Wilde once said, "*I can resist anything but temptation*". Remove the temptation so that you can resist it.

This discussion on the clean-up process begins with three assumptions, which must be used to guide your restructuring activities. The first assumption is highlighted in the following example. A smoker who has a cigarette in the house is more likely to relapse than somebody who has to walk to the shop to get a cigarette. Therefore, anything that makes it harder to access the cigarettes, or in this case pornography, has to be of benefit. Delay is a helpful part of being able to surf the urges.

The second assumption is that we live in a world of technology and therefore need computer equipment. It may be helpful in dealing with pornography to disconnect the Internet, but that can have other ramifications in your life. You have to master the technology not simply eliminate it.

The third assumption of behavioural management is that irrespective of how much you clean up your world, only self-control is completely effective. There are always other ways of accessing information (such as mobile phones, work computers, hotel Internet systems) which can trip you up. Therefore, at best this is about trying to maximise the opportunities to make it harder for yourself, rather than trying to eliminate all possible situations.

The first part of the clean-up requires you to have considered your use patterns. When are you using your computer for productive purposes and when are you most at risk of the pornography problem? Do you use the computer inappropriately at night-time, in the morning, at home, at work etc.? Once you are aware of when and how you are using the computer, you can begin the clean-up process.

The second step is to eliminate any pornographic material you have in the house. Delete pictures and movies from hard drives, and destroy collections. Erase your favourites menu from your computer browser and clean out your browser history. Use software which prevents you from recovering the material if you need to, because I have seen people who have deleted and then recovered their material. In doing these things, you are effectively removing any existing supply of material so as to make it harder to access material quickly.

When cleaning up do not forget to consider material you may have hidden in different places, such as the car, the garage, the office, on storage devices and spare USBs. It is critical to clean up computers, drives, cache memory and all other possible devices.

Some of you will find elimination quite hard because you have become attached to your favourite images. If you are resisting deleting the collection it may be a sign that you need professional help.

The third step of the clean-up is to examine your technology and determine what is necessary. You may argue that you need a computer at home to check emails and the news, but is that more important than overcoming your habit? Therefore, having a computer at work but not at home may be a partial answer. Decide on your priorities and put in place the necessary actions.

Software to control usage can be installed on computers. "Net Nanny" and similar programs can help to eliminate access to pornography. To do this you will need somebody else who can hold the password to prevent you access to the material. For the less sophisticated computer user, this can be a partial solution. I have found that some people with pornography problems are computer boffins and can easily get around these programs and password restrictions. Similarly, I have known of some people who moved from broadband to wireless broadband (the partner takes the USB stick to work). However, with the rapid use of the iPad and smartphones this might not be a solution for much longer. Tracking software allows another party to check your computer usage and send reports to a third party. As technology changes new variations of these tools will be developed.

Many of these techniques require the involvement of another person to monitor them. In a relationship there are plusses and minuses to having your partner involved. The last thing we want is for your partner to become your police officer, because it will add to the problems already in the relationship. The downside of any strategy involving other people is that it is only a partial solution – ultimately self-control is the only effective control. I had a client who encouraged his wife to look after his laptop, and then he would go looking for it. He would blame her for letting him find it. This is a good example of him not taking responsibility for his problem.

I have recently been reading about software which can be used to manage time on the computer. Once set, it only lets you access certain programs at certain times. Such technology can be useful as long as you are not able to override it.

There are a variety of functional ways in which you can rearrange your life. Move the computer from the home office to a public area in the house, or make new rules for the computer. To explain using a common relapse scenario: Somebody has been doing very well in their treatment program. They check an email which is an advertisement for holidays, including a picture of a bikini-clad woman. The image triggers thoughts about searching the Internet and away they go because at night it is possible to access the computer.

Having a rule to check the computer in the morning but not at night can safeguard against some of the slip-up behaviours, because a majority of you look at pornography at night (although patterns of behaviour are as varied as people's lifestyles). Conversely, if the computer is in a public area, you are not going to follow the image of the bikini-clad woman if the computer is in the same room as your partner or children or if you need to rush to work.

The issue is to make the environment work in your favour rather than in a way that encourages inappropriate use. As technology becomes smaller and more portable these solutions will be harder to implement. For example, I used to recommend to parents with teenage pornography users to have the computer in the lounge room. These same teenagers can now look up pornography on their smart phones in their bedroom. It is easier to hide a smart phone than a computer.

Key Points

- It is important to clean out everything that is likely to trigger some thought or reaction leading to pornography viewing, or which can be used to make the problem happen. Delay is a helpful part of being able to manage the urge.

- We live in a world of technology and most people need computer equipment. You have to master the technology, not try to eliminate all of it.

- Irrespective of how much you clean up your world, ultimately self-control is the only completely effective means of management.

- Do a thorough clean-up of all of your pornography and consider how best to structure the use of your computers.

- In a relationship there are plusses and minuses to having your partner involved. If your partner is now your police officer it will add to the problems already in the relationship and shifts the responsibility from you to them.

- There are functional ways in which computer use can be rearranged to make it harder to view pornography. Examine your pattern and see what you can do.

Exercise 39 – The Clean-up

You need to make a firm decision to eliminate all of the inappropriate material from your world. Be sure that you are ready because saving some of your favourite material will only lead to problems later. When you are ready, do the following:-

- Eliminate all pictures and movies stored on your computer, hard drives and other media.

- Remove any hidden material stored elsewhere.

- Examine the need for computers at home and find ways to make it work most effectively, including time and place.

- Examine whether a technological solution, including a "Net Nanny" type of program, is going to help.

- Review the discussion in the previous section to ensure that you cover as many solutions as possible.

Time Management

Kimberley Young, one of the pioneers into the study of Internet addiction, highlights the importance of strategies for time management, because it has been found that one of the most common problems for the Internet user is that they are consistently out of control in their use of time. He and various co-workers argue that moderation and controlled use of the Internet in general is a central part of the recovery process. Young argues strongly that time management techniques that help you to recognise, organise and manage time spent online, coupled with techniques which improve off-line activities, are a central part of the treatment process.

Results from surveys of Internet addiction show that patients reported that online time management was the most difficult aspect, followed by relationship problems and sexual problems due to a lessening of interest in real-life partners because of the preference for online activities. Consequently, the time management aspect is a critical component of the recovery process.

The logic in their recommendation is central to the recovery process. While abstinence from pornography may be necessary to prevent the reactivation of the associated pornography highway, most of you will still need to interact with computers and engage in online activities. Similarly, learning to stop at any time is a critical skill which has been lost to most compulsive users.

As you slide down the funnel, it is often the long periods of continuous online activity which gradually overrides your defences and allows you to engage in the inappropriate behaviour. Therefore, learning to manage your time on the computer is imperative. In a separate section I discussed some of the practical strategies in reorganising the way the computer is used around the home. In this section there are several important principles which need to be learnt. The first of these is the ability to develop a new and healthy routine, and to develop positive alternative experiences.

One of the techniques advocated by Young is based on practising the opposite; that is, making you break your current Internet routine to develop a new and more adaptive behavioural pattern. For example, if you go online as soon as you arrive home from work and remain online until you go to bed, you need to introduce a structured break for dinner and to watch the news, and only then return to the computer. On the one hand this reduces the total time online, but more importantly it begins to break the large continuous block into smaller pieces. See the exercise below for practice (Exercise 40 – Practicing Opposites).

The second technique is to use external stopping devices in which an alarm clock is set for periodic breaks. Similar to the way in which airlines suggest that you exercise every 30 minutes to prevent blood clots, you break continuous larger blocks of usage on the computer into smaller blocks of time. There are various types of alarms on most modern phones (periodic alarms, timers, and count-down timers) which are easily programmable. It is possible to set the alarm for particular activities, such as dinner or bedtime, as well as to signal regular 15 minute breaks and longer breaks every two hours. Without an external warning those of you who are engaged in the intensity of the online experience have a distorted perception of time and find that it is hard to self-monitor.

Coupled with these micro techniques is the need to be able to plan the use of your time in your life. To use time effectively you need to work out how you want your life to run, including how much time you would like to be online during a week. In addition, your plan needs to cater for basic functions such as bedtime (to avoid the sleep deprivation referred to earlier), dinner time, and other important breaks. Exercise 42 explains how to create a time management structure.

The structuring should be done prior to the start of the week. This allows you to schedule and reschedule. This is where the earlier exercises about what you want to do with your time come into play (especially "Finding New Friends"). The replacements for your lost friend have to make their appearance now.

The activity at the end of this section (Exercise 42 – Time Planner) is to help you to refocus on how to put those things that need to be in your life back into your day-to-day thinking. It is important to have positive experiences and I am yet to meet somebody who suffers from any compulsive behaviour who hasn't sacrificed other areas of their life.

Key Points

- Online time management, followed by relationship problems and sexual problems are some of the most significant problems arising from online pornography usage.
- Time management is a critical component in the recovery process.
- Micro time management in the form of being able to take breaks from the computer rather than staying continuously online, is important for regaining control. Set regular breaks.
- Macro time management for daily routines is critical. For example, set your bedtime before starting to use the computer.
- Overall life management is central to recovery. The way in which use your time is critical for effectively developing new neural pathways.

Exercise 40 – Practising the Opposite

The opposite to spending continuous blocks of time on the computer is to have a break. Start putting regular breaks in place. For example, if you go online as soon as you come home and remain online until you go to bed, introduce a structured break for dinner and to watch the news, and only after that go back to the computer. On the one hand this reduces the total time online, but more importantly it begins the concept of breaking the large continuous block into smaller units.

Exercise 41 – External Alarms

Schedule breaks by setting an alarm. If you use the computer recreationally, there should be one longer break of least 15 minutes every 2 hours, and short breaks of about 5 minutes every 20 minutes. Start structuring your time so that you have short regular breaks, longer breaks, and a productive use of your time.

Exercise 42 – Time Planner

Take a blank sheet of paper, turn it on its side (landscape) and draw a narrow margin followed by 7 equal columns across the page (alternatively print a page using Google calendar in week view). In the heading of each column, write the day of the week. In the left-hand margin, write the hours from midnight through to midnight equally down the page. In other words, set up a schedule which can show every day of the week broken down into hours.

Think about your last week, or alternatively a typical week. Using a highlighter pen, shade from the time you started on the computer to the time you finally went to bed. This page will have a number of highlighted areas. As you look at the shaded area, first of all ask yourself whether there is any pattern? Are there any particular days, times or locations which seem to trigger the use? If there are, go to the relevant sections in this book, such as the section on triggers, to see what you can do to deal with the pattern of use.

Draw up a new weekly schedule with the same timelines and show what you would your week to look like. This time ensure that you write in your scheduled activities you committed to undertaking in the Finding New Friends exercise (Exercise 38).

Place this revised schedule near your computer. When you start the Internet, use the principles from the two previous exercises to manage your time. Schedule a break of at least 15 minutes every 2 hours, and 5 minutes every 20 minutes, using an alarm clock or some other means. Start structuring your time so that you have regular breaks, longer breaks and a productive use of your time.

Consequences

I do not have to tell you that the pornography problem is causing you problems in your life. You know that better than anyone. For many of you, thinking about it makes you feel shame and guilt. If that is you, chances are you are using the consequences to beat yourself up each time you have engaged in the behaviour. This section is about learning to use the consequences in ways to help you, rather than to damage your sense of self-esteem.

Some guilt over your behaviour is useful. If you do not feel bad about something, why change it? The only people who have no guilt are people who feel no wrong, so they are psychopaths, narcissistic, or people who for some reason or other do not consider that what they are doing is wrong. Therefore guilt can be a motivator if used in the right manner.

Motivational interviewing is a technique in the alcohol and drug area which helps people to identify the pay-offs from getting over the behaviour, and the consequences from not getting over it. It has some useful techniques which you can apply to your problem.

Most of you with addictions think about the consequences <u>after</u> the event, so it makes you feel bad. Ironically, feeling bad makes you more inclined to relapse into the addiction to escape your bad feelings. The trick is to learn consequential thinking so that you consider the consequences <u>before</u> the behaviour. If the urge is rising and you start thinking about how it would impact upon you, then you are more motivated to stop the action. One of my clients had a partner who was ready to leave if he continued his behaviour, so thinking about how it would impact his life if the relationship broke up, he increased his motivation to resist. Another man wanted to be involved in a church activity with his son but knew he would not be able to if he relapsed. He used these thoughts to motivate his resistance.

A number of people I have seen find it very useful to write on a small card, or have a screen on their computer, listing all the reasons they want to give up the behaviour (see Exercise 43 – Consequential thinking). It might be written in shorthand or code form so others do not necessarily understand what the list is all about, but it simply identifies the benefits of doing the right thing, and highlights the consequences of doing the wrong thing.

According to behaviour therapy, conditioning is also taking place as a consequence of the behaviour. To understand conditioning, we can now put together various parts of the discussion we have had to date. The powerful emotions and chemicals associated with viewing pornography, and especially the sexual climax, have a big impact on the way in which experiences are stored together in the brain. The brain is designed to reproduce those highly pleasurable experiences and the positive consequences are marvellous, otherwise the behaviour would not have become your friend. However, there is a set of learning factors which also take place, and that is the pairing of stimuli for triggers. A famous early study in Psychology, "Pavlov's dog", shows us that neutral stimuli can become triggered stimuli.

For those of you who are not familiar with this famous study, Pavlov studied the salivation responses of dogs. He introduced different food to see how much the dogs would salivate. However, he noticed that the dogs started to salivate at the sound of the footsteps of the person bringing the food. Therefore, he set up some ingenious experiments in which food delivery was preceded by the ringing of a bell, and after a relatively few pairings of the bell before the food, the dogs would start to salivate simply at the sound of the bell. This became known as Classical Conditioning. In other words, the expectation of the consequence created powerful triggers.

My favourite example with the Internet is for those who have been around a little bit longer and are familiar with dial-up modems (before the day of broadband and wireless Internet). The computer used to make an interesting screeching noise. I had a number of male clients with an Internet pornography addiction who would find that just the sound of the computer logging-on would trigger a physiological arousal. This resulted from turning on the computer at night to begin a pornography session. The unintended consequence of this was they could be in a workplace and hear a computer logging-on, and then get a strong physiological arousal (which at one level is embarrassing, but on another level would trigger the thoughts and desires to look at material on the computer).

An understanding of classical conditioning can be used to help deprogram triggers, which will be discussed in the next section.

Key Points

- Some guilt over your behaviour is useful. If you do not feel bad about something, why change it?

- The only people who have no guilt are people who feel they do no wrong, meaning they are usually psychopaths, self-centred, or do not consider that what they are doing is wrong.

- Most people with addictions think about the consequences after the event so it makes them feel bad. The trick is to learn consequential thinking so that you consider the consequences before the behaviour occurs.

- The expectation of the consequence creates powerful triggers. This can be used to help deprogram certain problematic behaviours.

Exercise 43 – Consequential Thinking

Draw two columns on a small card. In the first column write all the problems associated with the behaviour, and in the second column write all the benefits from giving up. Make sure you note all the big impacts in your life.

If necessary write it in a shorthand or code form so that others do not necessarily understand what the list is all about.

Place this card in your wallet or some other place for easy review. It can be used in conjunction with the safety plan (Exercise 34 – Escape Plan). In other words, on the escape plan card, include an item which says to read this card.

7
Important Treatment Strategies

Paradoxical Keys to Change

The name of this section was designed to get your attention. The paradox is that the very behaviour that causes the problem can also be used to fix the problem. In other words, masturbation can help restructure triggers. I would like all of you, religious or otherwise, to review this section because of its importance to the more significant end problems.

The Sex Addiction Workbook by Sbraga and O'Donahue has an excellent section on the use of masturbation to assist with the treatment of sexual problems. However, I believe that the section is lost in their book as it has not been flagged as very important. The fact you are reading this section on using alternative methods to resolve the problem, means that I have your attention.

Masturbation is a self-directed action which gives rise to a huge range of opinions. My wife wanted to call this book "*stop it or you will go blind*"! This reflects one set of old fashioned attitudes. There are plenty of you who have no problem with the idea of masturbating, and see it as helpful. Others of you may be very religious and define such attitudes as abhorrent. If you are in the latter group, I am not seeking to change your beliefs. I would instead like to help you work within your beliefs, so please read what I have to say before moving to another section.

Masturbation and pornography addiction go hand in hand for many but not all users. For many of you, both religious and secular, it is not a question of whether or not to do it because it is already a part of the process for most of you. The sexual release associated with the action is often the exit to the tunnel. As explained earlier, the powerful feelings and chemicals associated with this reinforce the fantasies and attractions. It can be a significant reason for the way your attraction to certain types of images was formed.

For the religious minded, the ideal aim is for a healthy functioning relationship with a partner. If you are going online excessively, especially if you are having inappropriate fantasies, you have a major problem. Masturbation can be used in several ways on the journey back to recovery (Exercise 45). If you have inappropriate fantasies it can be used to help you retrain your mind to get it back on track. Similarly, a quick release of sexual tension has to be an improvement over 2 or 3 hours of searching, particularly if masturbation follows anyway. I see it as the lesser of two evils – to use a 5 minute release to avoid hours of inappropriate fantasy.

In my opinion, it is also the lesser evil to use masturbation for a temporary period, in some specific therapeutic ways, to eliminate inappropriate fantasies from your mind. If after reading this section you feel it is not for you, I have some other strategies (not masturbation based) to help you to achieve a similar outcome.

Masturbation can be used as an aid to self-control in three main ways. First, it is a way of bringing yourself to an orgasm, for sexual gratification, to release sexual tension, and as a distraction from other experiences. Second, it can be used to strengthen sexual fantasy, especially when used as means of developing healthy sexual fantasies. Third, it can be used to decrease arousal for dangerous or inappropriate fantasies.

The first use of masturbation is consistent with the highway model. If there are sexual tension triggers, quick release with minimal use of any fantasy will stop the pathways from being activated. This is an essential strategy if you engage in risky behaviour with real people. If you have just masturbated, you are unlikely to pay for a prostitute or try to meet someone over the Internet. For those whose belief systems allow it, it is an easy way of getting rid of sexual tension.

The second use of masturbation is related to the strong feelings associated with sexual release. We know that the fantasies and behaviours present at the moment of sexual release are powerfully connected. Fantasy is a necessary part of healthy functioning. We like to create fantasies of what we would do to escape the drudgery of day-to-day life if we won Lotto. We fantasise about lying on the beach during times of stress. Sexual fantasies make relationships fun and exciting. The key is to have appropriate fantasies about your real partner.

For someone with a pornography problem, one of the disadvantages of sexual fantasies is they reactivate the neural pathways. In my opinion, over time, repetitive feelings of sexual release have programmed the particular fantasy to become something quite inappropriate. There may be a very narrow range of stimuli which are extremely exciting. Some of you might be attracted to child pornography, to actions such as cum-shots on the face, or other inappropriate stimuli. My argument is that there is a need to try to restructure the fantasy into something appropriate. The most appropriate fantasy object should be your sexual partner. If you do not have one, you will need to address those relationship issues. If you do have a partner, it is important that your partner is arousing to you. In the earlier exercises, in which you identified the sort of images that were arousing to you, the greater the disparity between a sexual partner and that fantasy, the harder the sexual relationship will be, and the greater the reliance upon inappropriate sexual fantasy.

The explanation provided earlier about the way in which attraction becomes paired through the sexual experience is the key to getting out of that situation. There are a handful of psychological techniques which can help shift the fantasy. The first of those is called "Arousal Reconditioning" (Exercise 45). You begin with your preferred stimuli until aroused, and then when the arousal is strong you consciously swap to the appropriate fantasy. For example, if you are attracted to images of young teens, you may start with that image and then switch to an image of a healthy adult partner as sexual arousal increases. While some of you may find that technique effective, especially if it is hard to become aroused using a real partner, the downside is that for a period of time you are reactivating the unwanted pathways.

The second type of approach has the lovely name of "Orgasmic Reconditioning" (Exercise 46), which involves gradually decreasing the frequency of the deviant masturbatory fantasies and increasing the frequency of normal fantasies at the point of orgasm. In this case, you use conscious processes to think about the positive stimuli, being very mindful that all thoughts need to follow the positive purpose.

An important aspect of sexual functioning is the fact that after orgasm there is a period when men cannot function sexually. This period, called the refractory period, includes a recovery time during which it is physically impossible to have another erection, and a psychological period of satiation. Satiation means that, if you were in a desert without water on a very hot day, you would give almost anything for that first glass of water. However, after you have 3 glasses, your interest begins to wane. When you have had 20 glasses of water, you may reach a point where you are not interested in drinking any more, even if someone paid you to do so. This is the point of complete satiation.

This then leads to an approach that is very useful for anyone who has deviant fantasies. Masturbatory Satiation (Exercise 47) works with the orgasmic reconditioning to increase positive fantasy. Allow yourself to reach orgasm

Important Treatment Strategies 195

with the appropriate real person or fantasy in mind. Once the exciting feelings have past, swap to an inappropriate fantasy and try to masturbate now that you are physically limp and in the satiated period. It is critical you swap to the appropriate fantasy if you begin to become aroused. More detailed instructions are included below.

For those of you who are opposed to masturbation, the *Sex Addiction Workbook* includes a technique called Verbal Satiation (Exercise 48). While alone, describe the deviant fantasy out loud for twenty to forty minutes, three or more times per week. You talk through the scenario exactly as it comes to mind. You may want to record the fantasy and replay the tape, before making a new fantasy. If you have the sexual fantasy at a time other than during the session in which you talk about the fantasy, try to keep an appropriate person or action in mind. If you keep talking about the inappropriate fantasy, it eventually loses its interest and new fantasies appear less frequently.

The final techniques are called "Aversive Conditioning" (Exercise 49) and "Covert Sensitisation" (Exercise 50). Aversive conditioning has been used with some sex offenders, but it is what I refer to as a technique of last resort or a technique of desperation. If the fantasies you have are extremely reprehensible to you, then it may be worth experimenting with this technique. Basically the technique works by pairing the fantasy with a negative experience. The easiest negative experience is to use a small bottle of a very unpleasant smelling substance, such as ammonia. Waft the smell under your nose (but not too closely!) when the fantasies occur so that after a while the fantasy is paired with an unpleasant stimulus. Be careful that the substance you use is not taken in toxic doses. I stress that this is an approach of last resort.

Another variation is covert sensitisation (Exercise 50). Here you use the breathing technique discussed earlier (Exercise 28). When you are as relaxed as possible, visualise the fantasy that could lead you into trouble. Consider the deviant fantasy and, at the moment the fantasy is most exciting, visualise a very unpleasant thought in as much detail as possible. For example, imagine yourself looking at pictures on the Internet and getting very excited over some images. Just as you picture yourself about to masturbate to the images you are watching, think of something terrible (such as your dog vomiting over your feet, the smell of the fresh vomit, and your computer shorting out due to the power board getting wet with the vomit). You need to fine tune the disgusting part to suit your own dislikes, whether it is based on sight, sound or smell.

All of these techniques have a potentially powerful impact. However, if you are not able to achieve the desired effects, seek professional assistance. While professionals will use the same techniques, it is often only a minor variation in the process which can make the difference between success and failure.

Key Points

- Masturbation can be used as an aid to self-control in three main ways. First, it is a way of bringing yourself to an orgasm, for sexual gratification, to release sexual tension, and as a distraction from other experiences. Second, it can be used to strengthen sexual fantasy, especially when used as means of developing healthy sexual fantasies. Third, it can be used to decrease arousal for dangerous or inappropriate fantasies.

- For the religious minded, masturbation to release tension early may be the lesser of two evils. If you were going to end up masturbating following hours of activating the neural pathways, early release is better.

- A range of techniques has been developed to help change fantasy stimuli. The key element is to ensure that what you think about at the point of orgasm needs to be an appropriate fantasy.

Exercise 44 – Sexual Tension Release

If there are sexual tension triggers, quick release by masturbation with minimal use of any fantasy will stop the pathways from being activated. It is better to act early than to end up in the same place later. This is simply a case of using masturbation without imagery or fantasy to quickly reduce the sexual feelings.

For those of you who are religious, this could be seen as a bridging process with the eventual goal of eliminating the masturbation altogether. However, in the short to medium term, it can be helpful as it allows you to first eliminate the bigger problem of the Internet. In other words, minimise guilt by seeing that there is a greater good in the future.

For anyone engaging in dangerous or illegal behaviour, masturbation should be a part of your safety plan. Release the sexual tension rather than act on a plan which results in hurting someone in a sexual way. It is better to act early than allow a build-up of tension.

Exercise 45 – Arousal Reconditioning

This is the first of several techniques used to change fantasies towards ones involving an appropriate person and activity. The essence of these techniques is that the brain needs to pair the appropriate fantasy with strong sexual feelings.

Arousal reconditioning uses arousal feelings to train your brain to be excited by things you <u>want</u> to be aroused by. You begin by thinking about your preferred image, getting you excited until aroused, and when the arousal is strong you consciously swap to the appropriate fantasy. For example, if attracted to young teens, you might start with that image and then switch to an image of a healthy adult partner who cares about you. It takes effort to ensure that you stay focussed on the image you want. If thinking about the appropriate fantasy causes you to lose your erection, then you may have to commence the process again. The goal of this technique is simple – become aroused to the things that are good for you, but use the inappropriate fantasy to start the arousal if the appropriate fantasy is not arousing you enough.

Exercise 46 – Orgasmic Reconditioning

Orgasmic Reconditioning builds on the approach of Arousal Reconditioning in that the goal is to use the intense arousal of orgasm as the pairing factor for the brain (rather than general arousal), while ensuring that the fantasy or thoughts at the point of orgasm are an appropriate sexual image.

The process involves using an appropriate fantasy to bring yourself to near orgasm, then rest briefly to let the near orgasm feeling fade before repeating the pattern. Therefore, there are short cycles of arousal to near orgasm and then a rest. Eventually allow yourself to go to orgasm, however, you must hold the correct fantasy in your mind at that point (for example, the healthy image of the adult who cares about you).

Some people with strong fetishes find that they cannot achieve arousal with an appropriate fantasy (the preferred option) so the alternative is to use the inappropriate fantasy to become aroused, switching the image at the point of orgasm.

Make sure that you use sexual positions and practices which are within the normal range of your sexual activity. Simply changing the person while thinking about extreme acts is not sufficient to develop the changes you are trying to achieve.

Exercise 47 – Masturbatory Satiation

Begin with the orgasmic reconditioning exercises to increase positive fantasy. Allow yourself to reach orgasm with the appropriate real person or fantasy in mind. You will therefore masturbate to near orgasm a few times with the healthy adult fantasy and then ejaculate to that image.

Once the exciting feelings have passed, swap to the inappropriate fantasy to which you will now masturbate. Note that you are now limp and in the satiated period. A period of up to 45 minutes should be used to masturbate to the inappropriate fantasy. As it is the refractory period, it is not an exciting time and it takes effort to stay focussed. Please try to do it for the full 45 minutes. In other words, if your inappropriate fantasy is young teenagers, think about young teen images while trying to masturbate without an erection.

You may need a little oil or lubricant to prevent chaffing but perseverance is essential. Three sessions per week would be optimal.

It is critical that you swap to the appropriate fantasy if you begin to become aroused. For example, if after masturbating without erection to the young teen image you feel arousal coming on, think about the adult image again.

The technique can work with fantasy and real images. For example, do not use pornography to reach ejaculation (Orgasmic Reconditioning part of the process), but view the portions of clips which have previously been arousing while masturbating in the satiated period.

Exercise 48 – Verbal Satiation

For those opposed to masturbation, the *Sexual Addiction Workbook* includes a technique called Verbal Satiation. You need to be alone and describe the deviant fantasy out loud for twenty to forty minutes. It is important to do this in as much detail as possible. Talk through the scenario exactly as it comes to mind. You may want to record the fantasy, and replay the tape before making a new fantasy. In other words, if your fantasies involve oral sex with young teens, talk them through.

This exercise should be repeated three or more times per week. If you have the sexual fantasy at a time other than during the session in which you talk about the fantasy, try to keep an appropriate person or action in mind.

Exercise 49 – Aversive Conditioning

Aversive conditioning has been used with some sex offenders and with people who have fetishes. It has been found to work but, because it uses unpleasant means, it is not seen as an ethical way of treating conditions. I have included it as an option so that you can weigh up the appropriateness of using a negative technique. Therefore, it is what I call a technique of last resort, or a technique to be used in desperation when all others do not work. If the fantasies you are having are extremely reprehensible to you, then it could be worth experimenting with this technique. Basically the technique works by pairing the fantasy with a negative experience.

The easiest negative experience is to use a small bottle of a very unpleasant smelling substance, such as ammonia. Waft the fumes under your nose (but not too closely!) whenever the fantasies occur, so that after a while the fantasy is paired with an unpleasant stimulus. Be careful that the substance you use is not taken in toxic doses.

A similar variation is to use a rubber band on the wrist (be careful not to use one that cuts off your circulation). Each time you have an inappropriate fantasy ping the elastic.

I stress that this is an approach of last resort. For example, if you have sexual thoughts involving children, as soon as the thoughts start, waft the fumes or ping the rubber, then try to stop the thought or distract yourself from it.

Exercise 50 – Covert Sensitisation

Begin with the breathing technique discussed earlier (Exercise 28). When relaxed, visualise the fantasy that could lead you into trouble in as much detail as possible. The deviant fantasy will be considered for a short while. Then, at the moment when the fantasy is most exciting, visualise a very unpleasant thought in as much detail as possible.

For example, picture yourself looking at a movie on the Internet and getting very excited over some images. Just as you picture yourself about to masturbate to the images you are watching, think of something terrible (such as your dog vomiting over your feet, the smell of the fresh vomit, and your computer shorting out due to the power board getting wet with the vomit).

You need to fine tune the disgusting part to suit your own dislikes, whether it is based on sight, sound or smell.

Sexuality

Sexuality is inescapably linked to Internet pornography problems. The two essential parts of knowledge are first to understand how repetitive viewing of pornography impacts upon sexuality, and second to develop the capacity for a healthy sexual relationship.

In considering the nature of pornographic pictures and videos, it is important to remember that this material derives from an entertainment and media business. By entertainment, I mean that there is tremendous effort put into understanding how it works. Research has also been devised to determine what men like. The Internet is the perfect vehicle for helping to determine what does and does not work, because any provider of web material can log the number of hits on each image, how long videos were viewed for, which images or videos were downloaded etc. Therefore, popular material can be re-created and extended, and less popular material can be relegated elsewhere.

Furthermore, the Internet has been a wonderful medium for developing images related to specific fantasies. Every website has an index, perhaps more appropriately described as a "menu", to allow you to find just the right sort of images. Whether you like big-breasted or small-breasted women, whether you want to watch cum-shots on faces, or have a preference for blondes or brunettes; it is all there, categorised and ready for the taking. It is a smorgasbord for the sexually hungry, with tasty morsels for all appetites.

The business aspect relates to the fact that pornographic videos are produced by a movie making business.

The experience is largely not real. When you watch a movie you see a sexual encounter which goes for some 20 to 30 minutes, involves a variety of different sexual poses, and finishes up typically with ejaculation on the woman involved. Without going into too much detail, it is easy to see why these things take place. First, the external ejaculation provides a visual image – it loses its effect if the so-called "money" shot occurs internally rather than externally. Second, through the use of a variety of poses, it provides for a range of fantasies (oral, anal, vaginal, front, back, top, bottom, etc.) in every movie. There is something in each movie for a wide variety of viewers. The greater the number of viewers they can please, the more downloads they can achieve. Finally, many aspects of what you see can be a compilation. A movie does not have to be made in a single setting; the sequence may be carried out over several days. Therefore, the whole experience is an artificial view of a sexual encounter.

This creates a real dilemma for people who continuously watch it, and especially for young people without any knowledge of a healthy sexual experience. Our education system does not tell us how to have a healthy sexual relationship. Young people are told how to have safe sex, but they are not necessarily informed about moral attitudes or responsible relationships. Therefore, a lot of their learning comes from watching pornography. Herein is the fundamental problem, in that the videos are designed to reflect what men like, involving men getting their pleasure and women doing what men want. In real healthy sexual relationships, the two parties both need to have their desires met. The experience does not usually consist of 20 to 30 minutes of sexual contact, and it should have a courtship element (which is often not portrayed in pornography). When normal sexual activity is compared to pornographic movies (which are completely artificial), it creates a sense of inadequacy because you believe that you are not getting what you are viewing. You feel ripped off with the "boring" sex offered by your partner, and your partner feels like an object when you try to have the type of sex you have been watching.

The material is designed to be arousing and one way of making it arousing is to make it hard-core. Therefore, a number of practices that appear frequently in these movies are quite arousing for men (for example, anal sex). While some women might enjoy anal sex, the vast majority are quite reluctant to engage in it or are even appalled by it. When you view a lot of pornography, you may want to try some of what you've seen in your relationship. In my experience, women frequently tell me that the more their partner views pornography, the worse their relationship becomes and the more objectified the women feel. You might feel inadequate because you are not getting what you think you are "supposed" to be getting. Therefore, satisfaction decreases because of this artificial and fabricated view of sexuality.

When one considers the actors used in the movies, a different set of false comparisons is possible. Typically a range of different women are portrayed, however, big-breasted is often seen as attractive (knowing that there are a range of preferences, movie makers do have an array of models). Lighting is adjusted to make the models more attractive, and movies can be touched up during production. Therefore, the female model is both more attractive and acts more erotically than is usual in reality. Similarly, the vast majority of male models tend to be over-endowed, which for many men can generate a sense of sexual inadequacy because they are comparing themselves to the exception, not the rule.

While there are a variety of different "stories" around the sexual encounter, the majority of sexual acts, especially in the "pornstar" domain, neither show loving contact nor reflect any type of intimacy. They simply show sexual positions. Most of the movies have dominance and control themes, and woman exist for the man's satisfaction. This does not reflect real life and therefore creates significant problems for couples.

Other aspects, such as the visual demonstration of ejaculation, create false assumptions. In a high number of "pornstar" movies, ejaculation occurs on the woman's face, mouth, or other parts of the body. Again, such behaviour is generally something most women find distasteful rather than enjoyable. Consequently, the more your views are shifted because of the pornography, the greater the disparity in satisfaction occurring within your relationship.

One exercise to re-establish a healthy sexual relationship is to re-learn how to relate to your partner sexually. Sensate focus exercises are commonly used in sex therapy. An Internet search can help you to find the basic elements of how to reconnect sexually with your partner using the sensate focus program. A modified version is provided below in the exercise on re-learning intimacy (Exercise 52). However, before engaging in this exercise, first read and consider the rest of this section.

When we consider the way in which sexual functioning works for men, as soon as you have ejaculated there is a period of recovery before you can function again. Sexual frequency varies markedly; however, when pornography becomes a problem the frequency of masturbation is often higher than the pre-existing levels of sexual function. For example, if you and your partner had been sexually active twice a week, but you are now online 5 times a week you will be completely depleted. The effect upon the sexual side of your relationship is that you will avoid sexual contact, preferring to use your artificial fantasies than your real partner. This creates relationship tension and added dysfunction.

Even if you masturbate only occasionally, you will start to make excuses to explain why you cannot perform, such as being too tired, too late or too busy. This of course then impacts upon your relationship. While some women are quite vocal about the impact upon the sexual side of their relationship, other women (who may not be as vocal about such issues) tell me that they are aware that their relationship has deteriorated.

For those of you who are not in a relationship, you run into real problems when you try to initiate a relationship. This is because your functioning is less than optimal and the things you want to do could be quite confronting to your partner. Your new partner may find your encounters rough and degrading rather than loving and fulfilling.

The net result of this is that, as with most pornography viewers who have a problem with their behaviour, you are likely to have problems with your sexual relationships. This can include a lack of capacity to please your partner due to your excessive masturbation; a desire for sexual practices which your partner does not enjoy; objectified views of your partner and sex; and a range of other issues.

Recovery ultimately entails developing a healthy sexuality. If you do not have a sexual partner, you will need to address the issues that are preventing you from forming a healthy and appropriate relationship. If you have a partner, and your online behaviour is frequent, then consider the exercise below called sexual holiday (Exercise 53). A sexual holiday does not mean going away for a dirty weekend! It means stopping all sexual activity for a period of time to allow the agitation on the neural highway to subside and a normal sexual drive to return.

Sexual performance and sexual functioning are two of the most difficult topics for couples to discuss. Even for those couples in close relationships, one of the most difficult topics to discuss is what each partner does and does not like sexually, and to be able to do so in a manner that does not cause offence. Our egos and sense of wellbeing are closely tied to how we view ourselves sexually. Consequently, it is critical to be able to explain and share what you need and how you need it. Sexual assertiveness is essential.

I have treated a number of men whose Internet addiction has developed because of difficulties relating to their partner. It is beyond the scope of this book to explain how to develop a healthy, functioning relationship, but you should seek assistance if you have experienced difficulties forming and keeping a relationship or developing a healthy, functioning pattern of behaviour. It will take time and effort, but the long-term benefits will be worth it. In my opinion, without a functional sex life, you will be unable to completely resolve your pornography problem. However, if your sexual interactions are not as frequent as you would like, it is important that you don't blame your partner for your problem. A basic communication strategy, useful for both relationship assertiveness and sexual assertiveness, is provided below (Exercise 54 – Assertiveness Skills).

Key Points

- Understanding the way in which repetitive pornography viewing impacts upon sexuality, and developing the capacity for a healthy sexual relationship, are essential parts of recovery.

- The pornography industry is an entertainment and media business. The visual images are an illusion of sexuality designed to appeal to fantasies, rather than to reflect real life.

- Pornographic movies are a carefully crafted artificial view of what a sexual encounter is like.

- A fundamental problem with pornography is that the images are designed to reflect what men like, involving men getting their pleasure from women doing what men want. In healthy sexual relationships, both parties need to have their needs met.

- The Internet is the perfect vehicle for creating fantasies. It is designed to be a smorgasbord for the sexually hungry.

- Pornography shows varied sexual positions and actions, not relationships.

- Women frequently report that they increasingly feel objectified and the quality of their sexual relationship declines as their partner's viewing of pornography increases.

- Most men with pornography problems also have problems with their sexual relationships. This can include a lack of capacity to please their partners due to excessive masturbation; a desire for sexual practices which the partner does not enjoy; treating their partners like objects; and a preoccupation with fantasies or fetishes, which are not normal for the relationship.

Exercise 51 – Journal Reflections

- Describe your sex life.
- Describe your partner's sex life. Have you asked her?
- Is your partner uninterested in the type of sex you like?
- How does this impact upon your relationship?

Important Treatment Strategies 211

Exercise 52 – Re-learning Intimacy
(based on Sensate Focus)

Pleasing a partner, while being able to express what pleases you, is an essential element of sexuality. Those of you who view pornography often become focussed on yourself instead of considering how to please your partner.

To learn what you like and how to please your partner, it is essential that you spend some uninterrupted time together to do some mutual sharing and re-learning (ideally, around 2 to 3 sessions per week for 3 weeks). If you are not comfortable with your body, or if you are uncomfortable talking about sexual matters with your partner, you may need the support of a therapist who has expertise in sexuality.

One of you should take the role of the toucher, and the other the role of the receiver. The roles will be swapped every seven to ten minutes, so that each of you has two turns. The first stage involves touching only (NOT on the genitals or breasts). Use some massage oil if you'd like to. The toucher explores all over other person's body using a variety of techniques (massaging or touching, using fingers or tongue etc.). The receiver must focus their attention on the sensations arising from the way in which he or she is being touched, giving feedback to the toucher as to what is or is not enjoyable. The receiver should also make suggestions on the way in which the toucher might improve his or her technique. There should be no sexual intercourse during or immediately after this session.

During the second week, the session continues in the same way, but the toucher is now permitted to make contact with the genitals and breasts (but no sooner than their second turn). As before, the receiver concentrates on his or her feelings and gives the toucher feedback on which forms of stimulation are nice and which forms are unpleasant. Arousal is likely, but these sessions should not involve sexual intercourse. At the end of the session, some masturbation, mutual or individual, may be necessary.

During the third week use the same process of alternating roles between toucher and receiver. The first turn should be body touching only; the second turn includes touching genitals and breasts; and the third turn can include sexual intercourse if you are both ready for this to occur. During this phase, it is advisable that you lie on your back with your partner on top in a straddling position. Hold the position so that each of you can enjoy the experience – thrusting is discouraged. Throughout this process, the receiver must guide and give feedback.

Please note that this is an abridged version of a program which has different variations. The essential element is that both of you re-learn what feels good without the pressure to perform.

Exercise 53 – Sex Holiday

For those of you with a high-level pornography problem and therefore are desensitised to normal sexuality, some treating practitioners recommend taking a sex holiday. This means ceasing all forms of sexual contact for a period of time (usually 2 to 4 weeks). This means no masturbation, no viewing of pornography, and no sex with anyone.

This exercise should be undertaken in conjunction with your partner, and you may need some therapeutic intervention, but if all sex is stopped for a period of time (that is, both sex with your partner, and Internet use) the "holiday" allows your brain to clear and gives sexual desire an opportunity to form a more normal pattern.

The next step is for you and your partner to begin to re-explore normal healthy sexual contact, which includes pleasing one another (see Exercise 52 – Re-learning Intimacy). You may need to have a period of time with no sexual contact, that is, time to learn to become intimate again. In this process, it is important for both of you to discuss your needs with one another.

This exercise will not have any benefit if you look at pornography at the same time. The pornography will distort your views of sexual relationships.

Exercise 54 – Assertiveness Skills

Good communication is a skill which can be learnt. If you'd like to improve your communication skills, both at work and at home, it is a good idea to read some of the readily available books on communication.

In the simplest model, the three components of communication are to define the problem behaviour, express your feelings with an "I" message, and explain the consequences of that behaviour.

For example, if your partner were to come home late, a typical response might be that *"you are selfish and inconsiderate, and you are always late!"* This could lead to an argument over either the name calling or whether or not your partner is always late. *"You are"* is blaming terminology. If you use *"you are"*, it could result in an argument. So what should you say?

Step one is to define the problem behaviour as it would be seen by an outside observer. *"You are always late"* should be stated as an objective fact such as *"you said you would be home at 6:00 pm, it is now 6:45 pm"*. The problem is defined and there is little room for argument.

Step two is to add the "I" message. *"I feel stressed and worried when you are late"*. It is hard to argue: *"no you don't feel that"*. An "I" message shows ownership of your feelings.

The final step is to explain two or more consequences of the problem behaviour. *"If you come home when you say you will, we would get on better. When you are late, we fight. If you could call so that I don't worry, I would feel more loving towards you"*. Here you have not told your partner what to do, but you have provided reasonable choices.

If you are going to practice assertiveness skills, start with small issues rather than large issues. Most people who have been passive (that is, not asking for their needs to be met) start by being too aggressive, which does not work. Practicing on smaller issues allows you to work up to the major points of discussion, such as sexual preferences.

Exercise 55 – Making Women Real

Women in pornographic movies exist to please the men in those films. It is not possible to avoid exposure to those objectified views of women, so you should try to make them real. Try asking yourself questions about the pornstars or actresses with a view to making them more real – to personalise those women. For example, questions that run counter to objectification might include, *"What are her relationships are like? What are her greatest life trials and struggles? What values and principles does she live by?"*

This exercise can be used in different ways. The exercise is best used early in the process of going online so that, instead of viewing images of women as objects of arousal, the actresses are seen as real people.

If you conduct some research into pornstars, you will discover that many of them were abused as children, or manipulated and exploited into the pornographic movie industry. Some of them have also suffered horrendous injuries from anal sex, or have caught diseases (for example, from going from anal to oral sex). It is not a glamour lifestyle leading to fame and fortune.

The Golden Key to Success

Until now I have provided you with facts, and exercises corresponding to those facts. All of this is useful, but you will need a structure for applying these strategies over a period of time if you want to make a difference in your life.

At this stage you need to realise that we are trying to cease both the behaviour and the urge which drives that behaviour. It is easier to stop the behaviour than to stop the urge, however, being aware of both the behaviour and the urge is your key to success.

The golden key which I share with you now is called the *"behaviour chain highway"*. The highway that I have discussed throughout this book takes place at one level of the neural pathways in the brain. However, at another level of these neural pathways, there is a series of choices and actions which create movement along the highway.

If you were solely the product of neural activity, you would not turn off the computer when your partner walks into the room, you would not stop viewing pornography for a period of time, nor would you do view pornography more frequently at other times – your behaviour would be an automatic pattern. You therefore have entrances onto and exits from the highway.

The key to this is to understand that the choices you make comprise a sequence which may take hours to put you onto the pornography highway. Consider the sequence below in Exercise 56 – Behaviour Chain Highway. In that example, the online behaviour did not start when the man's partner went to bed – it started with some mood-related experiences in the morning. Had those experiences been addressed, then the evening behaviour might not have taken place.

There are 60 exercises in this book which provide you with tools to manage the entrances onto and exits from the highway. This becomes most effective if you use any relapses to improve actions on the highway. In other words, the parts of the highway which have deteriorated will become stronger if you repair them. If on each relapse you can draw a detailed behaviour chain, you will be able to apply the appropriate exercise to each step on that chain. For example, some of the tools for the first 5 points in the behaviour chain in Exercise 56 include:-

1. Woke up late – time management, manage sleep.
   ↓
2. Rushed breakfast – calming skills from breathing exercise.
   ↓
3. Felt like an idiot – thought stopping, challenge thinking.
   ↓
4. Argued with partner – assertiveness skills / breathing exercise for calmness.
   ↓
5. Stopped at service station – preparation for entering a high risk environment.

Most of the links in the behaviour chain can be analysed and addressed. Even though a change may be simple or minor it can add up if it is linked with other small changes. Relapse, especially in urges rather than behaviour, is not a failure in the early to middle part of treatment, but is an essential element in the learning process. By paying careful attention to each time the urge is present, you can begin to make serious gains in your recovery.

If you are in therapy, it is useful to bring to the behaviour chain to your sessions to see if there are other ways of dealing with the problem behaviour. The chain comprises triggers, behaviours and consequences, which may be cyclic in nature.

The fact is that you will need to keep practicing these actions for the rest of your life. While a small number of you will eliminate the urge completely, most of you will have to manage your thoughts and feelings throughout your life. Will it be as hard later on as it is now? The answer is a resounding NO. After a period of time, you will have days, weeks and possibly months during which the urge and thoughts will be low level and only fleeting. However, from time to time, there will be triggers that might reignite those buried feelings.

During the early period of recovery, anything might cause a relapse because of the constant battle between good and bad choices. During the middle period of recovery, a relapse might be caused through carelessness – by letting your guard down too easily. You may have started well, becoming overconfident, which results in a slip-up. During the later period of recovery, a relapse is often caused by a significant life event which triggers a return to old patterns (for example, a relationship break-up, or a job loss might cause overwhelming stress).

When a relapse occurs, you will need to analyse the behaviour change which lead to that moment. Remind yourself that you can control your life in a meaningful way. Remind yourself of the terrible negative feelings that acting out generates. Be mindful of tolerating the feelings until they pass. Then recommit to living your life without the problem.

Key Point

- You are trying to cease both a behaviour pattern (viewing pornography) and an urge (the desire to view) which drives that behaviour. Stopping the behaviour is easier to do than stopping the urge. Understanding both is useful for regaining control.

- The "behaviour chain highway" on one level related to the neural pathways in the brain, but on another level it is a series of choices and actions which create movement along the highway.

- Most of the links in the chain can be analysed and addressed using the tools in this book.

- Relapse, especially in urges (rather than behaviour), is not a failure in the early to middle part of treatment, but is an essential element in the recovery process. Learn from it.

- During the early period of recovery anything might cause a relapse because of the constant battle between good and bad choices. During the middle period of recovery, a relapse might be caused through carelessness – by letting your guard down too easily.

> During the later period of recovery, a relapse is often caused by a significant life event which triggers a return to old patterns.
>
> - Some of you will eliminate the urge completely, but most of you will have to manage your thoughts and feelings throughout your life.
>
> - As time passes it will become easier to manage your behaviour. After a period of time, you will have days, weeks and possibly months during which the urge and thoughts will be low level and only fleeting.

Exercise 56 – Behaviour Chain Highway

Each thought and action is followed by another thought or action in a sequence or chain leading to an eventual outcome. During the early period of recovery, the links in the chain are often unclear, but they are critical points at which you can intervene.

One way of gaining insight into your personal dynamics is to draw a behaviour chain. Read the following example:-

1. Woke up a little late.
   ↓
2. Rushed breakfast, spilled cereal on shirt.
   ↓
3. Felt like an idiot.
   ↓
4. Argued with partner when going out the door.
   ↓
5. Car out of petrol, stopped to refill at service station, saw porn magazine in service station. Scanned magazine covers and saw an attractive blonde with large breasts.
   ↓

Important Treatment Strategies 221

6. Nagging thoughts about porn throughout the day after seeing magazine cover.
   ↓
7. Distracted at work because of the morning argument with partner.
   ↓
8. Occasional thoughts of porn to distract from thoughts of the argument.
   ↓
9. Boss was on your case at work because you were distracted.
   ↓
10. Felt annoyed at boss. Resentment rises.
    ↓
11. Started to think about going online later that night.
    ↓
12. Came home, felt moody.
    ↓
13. Evening not good as the argument was not discussed. Both of you are tense.
    ↓
14. Later asked partner for sex but she was not in the mood.
    ↓
15. Felt angry towards partner.
    ↓
16. Started computer, not to look at pornography but to check emails.
    ↓
17. Partner said it's time for bed, you said you'd be just a little longer.
    ↓
18. After a while you found yourself saying "stuff the bitch", consciously went to usual porn site.
    ↓
19. Looked at porn involving cum-shots on women who looked like your partner.
    ↓
20. Switched off all thoughts and spent around 2 hours in the tunnel.
    ↓
21. Afterwards felt guilty and angry at yourself.

The above chain has 21 steps in it. You should aim to identify at least 20 to 40 steps in the chain when you document it. Each time you engage in the behaviour, create a behaviour chain diagram to explain why the episode occurred. The information contained in the chain can be useful for the ABC model discussed in previous sections.

More importantly, if you see the chain of events leading to the pornography problem, you can view it as your highway. The details are a map of the highway which lead you to an unwanted destination. At each step, you can mentally block the on-ramp or build a new off-ramp. Ask yourself what you could do at each of the above 21 steps to avoid ending up at the destination. When looking for patterns, identify the common elements such as mood-related feelings, actions of others, or visual cues.

In the chain described above, it is significant that the actions from 18 onwards do not need to occur – that is, you can have an urge but not act on it. Managing the first 17 steps in the above chain is as important as managing the last three steps.

8

Other Important Points

Spirituality

A diverse cultural mix exists in the western world. In the USA, UK and Australia, the population predominantly consists of the mainstream Christian religions (Anglican or Catholic religions or their variants), but we also have significant sub-groups of both Christian and non-Christian denominations (Buddhists, Muslim, Hindi, Jewish, Latter Day Saints, Jehovah Witnesses, Baptists and many others). In Australia, only 15% of the population state that they do not have a religion, however, there is a difference between stating that you have a religion and being an active proponent of the faith. This section is directed towards those of you with a belief in God but, in particular, those who are active in within their religion. I hope that all of you, religious or otherwise, read this section.

The view that there is an ultimate ethical standard set by God is what separates the religious from the secular relates. Across the world, standards of morality are culturally determined (what the majority find acceptable) and individually based (whatever feels good in the privacy of your own home is okay). The secular members of the population are limited by laws prohibiting certain practices. For the religious, there is also an ultimate standard set by God, and violation of that standard has eternal consequences. Different religions and sects will view God's laws and standards in different ways, in accordance with the interpretation of the holy books of each of those different religions and sects.

The Porn Report noted that in almost all of the religious groups in Australia, pornography use was about the same, irrespective of religion. Whether or not you are a Christian, this will not stop you from using pornography. Your use of pornography might be slightly lower than for non-Christians, but it still exists. In my opinion, you are likely to have a greater degree of guilt over your behaviour because of the significant eternal ramifications. As explained earlier, guilt can be both destructive and motivating depending on how it is used.

Perhaps the clearest scriptural reference for Christians with respect to pornography can be found in Matthew 5:28 (King James Version) *"But I say unto you, that whosoever looketh on a woman to lust after her hath committed adultery with her already in his heart"*. Pornography really captures the meaning of that scripture, generating feelings of guilt.

We also know that child pornography is likely to be particularly bad in God's eyes: Matthew 18:6 *"But whoso shall offend one of these little ones which believe in me, it were better for him that a millstone were hanged about his neck, and that he were drowned in the depth of the sea"*. It is not intended that we act on these words in a literal sense, because we know that with repentance comes forgiveness; however, it indicates that child pornography is likely to be viewed as a serious issue. If you are in this category, please use the paradoxical keys to change – it is better to do what is necessary to change your behaviour than to stay in a vicious and destructive cycle. You should also seek help from both a professional and from your spiritual leaders.

From my observations, if you are a spiritual person, a cycle occurs when a pornography problem exists. The first component of this cycle, as discussed earlier, is based on the premise that most religions view pornography as something ranging from inappropriate to completely reprehensible (depending upon the interpretation of the scriptures). This view feeds guilt into the cycle (remembering, however, my earlier comments that guilt serves a purpose, namely, to correct wrong behaviour).

The second component of the cycle is that there is a difference between religion and spirituality. Spirituality is how much you feel the influence of God in your life, while religion is the practice of a particular faith. You can be religious and not spiritual (practice the rituals of your religion) or spiritual and not religious (some of the so-called new age religions do not follow formal practices but believe that God is in all of us). What this means is that everyone has a certain distance from God, that is, how close you feel to God or how strongly you feel your spirituality is particular to you. When you engage in something that conflicts with your fundamental beliefs it generates guilt and shame, which in turn results in you feeling guilty, anxious and/or depressed. You then become lonely and isolated because of these sorts of feelings. The pornography problem provides an escape to relieve you of these feelings, which then distances you even further from God. It is a downward spiral, because the worse you feel, the further you are from God, and the more attractive the escape strategies become.

Those of you who are highly religious often struggle with a binge pattern, rather than a constant use of pornography. A sense of righteousness causes tight control. You struggle to maintain appropriate boundaries, until the pressure reaches a crisis point at which time you binge for relief. Obsessive personality characteristics, the desire to present a righteous face to the world, and a building up of life pressures without an outlet makes this a very destructive pattern. Those of you who are more active members of a religion (including leaders such as priests, pastors or bishops), in particular, will struggle because you are caught in the cycle wherein you cannot disclose your problems for fear of what your flock will think of you. The pressure is high, creating a double life – a public face of good and a private world of sin – which is very emotionally destructive.

The alternative to the binge pattern is when, as a spiritual person, you feel so powerless from failed attempts to manage your urge, that you reach the point of feeling beyond help. If you have reached that point – feeling so powerless and fallen because of your unsuccessful attempts to give up, you may be indulging in the behaviour constantly. Worse still, depression and suicidal thoughts may also impact on your life. You believe that you cannot return to God, cannot find a way out of the pornography trap, and are eternally damned, so you think that there is no point in going on. In this state, you should not go it alone – you need the help of a good church leader and, if you have suicidal thoughts, professional assistance.

If you seek professional help, psychologists have an ethical requirement to respect your belief system and work from your perspective. Psychologists are required to respect the diversity and uniqueness of all people and you have the right to a linguistically and culturally appropriate service. A psychologist acknowledges people's right to be treated fairly and without discrimination or favouritism. If you feel judged by your therapist, it is best that you find another therapist who will work within your beliefs.

The ethical responsibility of psychologists is important because there are two ways for you to rid yourself of your shame. One is to change your religious beliefs, and the other is to change your behaviour. Which of these approaches is the most appropriate? There is possibly scope for a little of both, but ultimately it is the change of behaviour, rather than beliefs, which is the ethical approach. However, it is critical to determine whether your beliefs constitute the mainstream tenets of your religion. Within any church group, some people have distorted views of what their religion teaches. Are your beliefs a distorted view of your religious framework? Please ensure that you check with your spiritual leaders who are in the best position to advise you appropriately.

If the Church sees your behaviour as a sin, concepts such as confession and repentance are part of the healing process. However, you must find someone who will deal with you and your actions, without passing judgement upon you. You do not need to see a priest who views you as evil. You need help from someone who knows how to love the sinner while despising the sin.

Spiritually, repentance is the most powerful element in the process of recovery. In Acts 8:22-23 *"Repent therefore of this thy wickedness, and pray God, if perhaps the thought of thine heart may be forgiven thee. For I perceive that thou art in the gall of bitterness, and in the bond of iniquity"*. Being set free from the gall of bitterness, the promise of Christian religions, is a wonderful feeling. You are entitled to such outcomes if you get your life in order.

I have observed from years of working with church populations, that premature repentance is a problem. You repent and promise that you will never do it again. You feel that God forgives you – you cannot engage in the behaviour again. What a joy it would be if it was so simple. Unfortunately, when you relapse you feel a failure in God's eyes (and possibly also in the eyes of the religious leaders you were working with), so now you feel hopeless and powerless both personally and spiritually. To be free you may need to repent but, unless you find some tools to help you, you will spiral downward. The situation can be made worse by well-meaning but ill-informed people telling you that it did not work because you did not pray hard enough or repent properly.

It is important to use your religious tools, such as praying, fasting, or whatever else is used within your church. Praying is important. Daily prayers can help prepare your thoughts for the day. Prayer during times of temptation can help with the struggle. Add prayer to your relapse prevention card as one of the stages. Scripture study helps to create alternative pathways for the brain. Positive thoughts coupled with real repentance allows for forgiveness, which then builds self-esteem. This is the beginning of an upward spiral.

If you are a Christian, you need to remember that Jesus died for the remission of our sins, and ultimately there can be forgiveness. Matthew 26:28 *"For this is my blood of the new testament, which is shed for many for the remission of sins"*. The promise, if you get your life together, is that you can be reconciled with God. As you overcome your pornography problem you will feel an increase in spirituality and regain meaning in your life.

Key Points

- Religion is not a preventative for pornography problems. Users are found in almost all religious denominations.

- While the world views morality as relative, those who are religious have an absolute standard to follow – the standard set by God. Because of religious factors, feelings of guilt are higher for most users who are religious.

- Pornography causes people to feel distant from God. When the problem is active, the spiritual aspects of your life are impacted negatively.

- One of the common patterns for the religious user is the binge pattern. An attempt to apply control over internal thoughts and temptations, results in a feeling of being overwhelmed, and therefore a binge takes place.

- The alternative pattern occurs when all hope is lost, and the person feels that they will never be reconciled with God, so they let go of all control. Due to feelings of worthlessness, the behaviour becomes constant.

- Psychologists are required to work within the religious beliefs of their clients. Not all counsellors will do so, so ensure that you have someone to help you who will work within your framework.

- Working with a church leader for your spiritual recovery is helpful but not all leaders are equal in their approaches. Make sure that their beliefs are balanced (within church standards) and that their approach is to love the sinner and hate the sin.

- Use the spiritual tools available to you, such as praying, fasting and scripture study, as other means of help. Spiritual tools help to heal the spirit.

- Repentance is necessary for you to be free, but be careful of premature repentance where you feel like you have repented but do not have the tools for a complete change.

Other Important Points 231

Exercise 57 – Journal Reflections

- In your journal write about how the pornography problem has impacted on your spiritual wellbeing.

Exercise 58 – Integrating Spiritual Tools

The following list includes some spiritual tools for you to use when needed:-

- Make a list of all of the scriptures which give you help and courage to deal with your adversity. Review this list regularly, morning and night.

- Prepare a card listing the best scriptural references, and review these when you are feeling low.

- On your relapse card, include a step which involves prayer.

- On your daily planner include positive activities such as scripture study and daily prayer, as well as regular church attendance.

- Make a time to meet with your church leader to reconcile your problems.

- What other ideas do you have?

Partners and Their Reactions

Please do not skip this section dealing with the way in which your behaviours impact upon your partner. Unless you can understand what your partner needs, and why they react as they do, then you will put your relationship at risk. There is nothing that can compensate for the destruction of a family, so you owe it to both yourself and your partner to fix your relationship.

In my professional practice I work with families in Family Court separation proceedings, and I see no winners. The emotional turmoil of breaking up is one of the most common reasons for someone to seek professional help. The emotional pain, stress and depression associated with a break-up can push even a well-adjusted person to the limit. When children are involved, they suffer because of the loss of the family unit. Parents have significant grief issues which need to be resolved. If pornography is the reason for the break-up, it can have a significant influence upon the legal dynamics. Many of the players in the Family Court – lawyers, judges, counsellors – often do not understand the links between pornography viewing and risks to children, so some men end up having supervised visits with their children. To avoid these negative consequences, it is therefore important to fix the situation.

In this modern world, a "partner" can come in many different forms, however, most of the men I treat are heterosexual men with wives or girlfriends. This section is designed to address issues arising from a traditional sort of relationship and, in particular, the issue of cross-gender difference. If you are in a homosexual or another type of alternative relationship, some factors will be common to all parties, but there are different dynamics associated with your unique type of relationship. You may need to search the literature and seek advice specific to your relationship. I apologise for not covering issues related to all relationships, but there are limits to the range of topics I can address in this book (and research for the larger section of the population is in its infancy).

I would encourage you to share sections of this book with your partner. The more they understand about what you are doing and why, the more supportive they are likely to be. Ignorance generates fear, while knowledge lowers anxiety. Your partner probably knows less about your problem than you do. The first step is to help her to understand the model described earlier in the book, explaining why the problem happens. Sharing is the opposite of isolation. Exercises 54 and 59 will help you with this process. Note that too much detailed information may turn her off you, so be honest and frank in your disclosure, but be tactful.

As noted earlier, it is likely that you have problems with your sexual relationship. You cannot fix those sexual problems alone. Most women will stick by their partners if their partners are serious about wanting to change. However, she will see through any superficial attempts to placate her by seeking help to keep the relationship. She does not want perfection, she wants honesty and effort. Women who have a good understanding of men's sexuality may be primarily concerned with the impact on her life because she has a disconnected and exhausted partner. She wants you to be there for her, not using the computer for many hours each night.

The less your partner understands male sexuality, the more they may have self-esteem issues about what you are doing, and the bigger their reaction because they feel personally rejected. It is seen as a type of visual infidelity when you choose to satisfy your needs with images of other women and not her. A tactless client told his partner *"not to worry about it as I only look at fat women"*. In his ignorance he thought he was placating her by saying his behaviour was not about her, and that it was something altogether different. From her point of view, she thought he was saying that she was not even as attractive as a fat woman!

Other women will consider that your family's moral values are being violated and placed at risk because of your actions. This is especially true if you are from a religious family or lifestyle. You may be seen as jeopardising the family's spiritual or emotional wellbeing. Instead of being the valued protector and provider, you are seen as a threat to the safety of the family.

More important than the impact upon sexuality, is the damage to trust. Many of my male clients were first referred to me because their wife or partner found out about the secret side of their life. A partner could have many reactions, but it is common for them to feel anger and betrayal from the violation of trust. If your behaviour has only recently been discovered, your partner may be feeling that they do not know who you are. It is an unnerving experience to be in a relationship with someone who has been secretly engaged in a pervasive pattern of behaviour. It challenges their sense of security about knowing who you are. They may see it as a dark and evil side of your makeup.

You have a problem if your partner has previously discovered your behaviour, and you promised to stop but didn't. They will doubt your capacity to stop and they will feel hurt because of your broken promises. A golden rule of recovery is to refrain from lying to yourself or to others. Trust can only come from honesty, however, as mentioned earlier, tact is also important. Your partner does not need to know every gory detail of every one of your inappropriate thoughts. A therapist is the person with whom you should share the fine details. Being honest can be hard, but the worst thing you can do is to say you have stopped and then get caught again. That damages the relationship more than admitting to the bad things in the first place. It is better to promise to try to change rather than to promise to cease forever (and fail to do so).

Explaining the process to someone of the opposite sex can be difficult due to differences in gender perceptions and experiences. Kastlemaine argues that there are gender differences with respect to the tunnel model. He says that most women report that they do not feel that they are so far in the tunnel that they have no choice. Women believe that they can always come out of the tunnel. Men will describe being in the tunnel as having a point of no return. Once they are in that state they do not feel that they can get out of it. They are locked into it. None of the women I have seen as clients, nor those in other cases I have read about, reported that the tunnel narrowed to the point where everything was blocked out. For men, the rest of their world will have disappeared during the tunnel stage. This reflects the way in which men and women will often deal with life in general, and the sexual experience in particular.

Although reporting that a climax is a part of the sexual experience, most women said that, when looking at pornography, climax is NOT the goal. Men look for 'the' image to achieve sexual release. Women say that they are not particularly interested in the images; the images are a just part of the total experience. Pornography for women is about the story, context and mood, not just the images. Men will generally tell you it is all about the images, however, they will also tell you that it is also about the emotional escape which comes from being online.

If you talk to women, some will see men's use of pornography as cheating. There are others who will see online chatting as a type of emotional infidelity. Many men do not see it the same way and are quite surprised when these issues are raised. Men will say that they are *"just looking"*, but a woman will believe that he would rather look at the images than her. The woman who feels like that will have her self-esteem impacted by your behaviour. Some men do not seem to understand that in real life, when sexual contacts take place (i.e. in the form of an affair), men will have an affair for sex, but women will generally have an affair for emotional reasons, such as love.

When we put these reactions into a package, your partner's feelings may run along the following lines: She will feel disgust and revulsion at the thought of what you are doing. She will not understand why you are doing it. She may feel a sense of betrayal. She may fear or worry about the future of your relationship and the safety of your children. The impact on her life will create anxiety. She will think about whether the relationship is going to work, whether you are going to leave for somebody else, and whether your children will see pornography because of your carelessness. She will feel jealousy, will wonder how she can compete, and all of this will affect her self-esteem. Your sexual relationship will get worse, not better. You might say that you were educating yourself, but your partner will feel like an object. She wants romance, while you want climax. As discussed previously, the impact on the sexual side of your relationship is huge.

When you discuss these issues with your partner, you need to be very careful that you do not let your partner get into denial, enabling or accommodating behaviour. It is very easy for women to make allowances for their partner, and in the process they inadvertently accommodate the dysfunction which drives the cycle. As your partner, it is critical that she knows that she has certain rights. You need to respect healthy boundaries, and she needs to be able to say 'no' to any sexual practices which she does not want to participate in. That is really important for trust and for rebuilding the relationship.

Partners might choose to watch a pornographic movie together, which is not a problem for many couples. If they watch videos from the video store, or look at magazines etc., there is a naturally occurring limit to the type of material that is included. The Internet does not have that limit, and that is where a problem can arise. It is not so much the content but the quantity of material. Some women take the approach that if they can't beat it, they will join it. They might watch some movies to please you, hoping that you will change. You then share some Internet pornography with her, and she is revolted by what she sees. Now rather than join you, she is against you.

Women need to learn that remorse is part of the cycle. As with domestic violence, there is a cycle of behaviour that is much like the wheel of violence. For example, you have the pornography problem but, when found out, you say you're sorry (very sorry), buy her flowers, promise to make up by behaving, then you view pornography again. Saying sorry means that you are being responsible, but it does not mean that you have changed. You have to learn to fix the problem. Women need proof of change, not just words.

The deception, as described earlier, is going to undermine your relationship until you can be honest again, including learning to be honest with yourself. If there are issues in your partner's past, these will reverberate. For instance, if your partner has a past history of being sexually abused, pornography is going to have a much bigger impact on her when she finds out than if she was a partner with a more liberal or accommodating attitude. So, you need to look at how her issues might reverberate.

It is important that you are honest in your relationship (to remove deception), that you make genuine attempts to change, and are respectful. If you can do these three things, most women will be supportive.

Key Points

- Your relationship is one of your most important assets. It is important that you seek to resolve the problems.

- Sharing the issues with your partner can elicit their support. However, it is your problem and you must take responsibility for your actions.

- Any sharing of what you are doing needs to be packaged with a liberal dose of tact.

- Most women will stick by their partners if their partners seriously want to change. However, she will see through any superficial attempts to placate her.

- From a male perspective they are just looking at images, however, for many women it feels like visual infidelity. You are choosing to satisfy your needs with images of other women and not with her.

- If your family has a religious focus, your actions will be seen to be jeopardising the family's spiritual or emotional wellbeing.

- Your partner could have one of many reactions, but feelings of anger and betrayal arising from the violation of trust are common. It is an unnerving experience to be in a relationship with someone who has engaged in a pervasive pattern of behaviour which has been kept secret.

- If your partner has discovered your behaviour before, and you promised to stop but didn't, she might now doubt your capacity to stop. Your partner will be hurting from broken promises.

- Two golden rules for recovery are: do not lie to yourself or to others, and never promise something that you cannot deliver.

- Women believe that they can always come out of the tunnel. Men will describe the situation as one of being in the tunnel and reaching a point of no return. Therefore it is hard for women to understand why men look at pornography and cannot stop.

Exercise 59 – Talking to Your Partner

It is a hard thing to raise issues with your partner if they do not know about the problem, but most women want to help someone they love. Some simple suggestions to help you talk to you partner are:-

- Timing – Pick a time when you will have adequate uninterrupted time to have a meaningful discussion.

- Context – If your partner is sick, tired, hormonal, busy or otherwise affected in her mood, leave the situation until she is happier.

- Facts – Describe what you have been doing in an assertive fashion (see Exercise 54 on assertive communication).

- Ownership – Use a lot of "I" statements, not "you" comments. "I" equates to ownership, while "you" equates to blaming.

- Answer questions honestly – Trust will be in an issue, so allow her to ask questions and take your time to answer.

- Promise wisely – Do not make promises you cannot keep. She may want you to promise never to do it again, but you can only promise to do all you can to fix the problem.

- Limits – Try to limit the discussion to one or two Key Points.

Protecting Society

Frederick Douglas said *"It is easier to build strong children than to repair broken men"*. I think that everyone, professional or otherwise, needs to educate the public about Internet pornography problems. I do not think that there are enough people talking about this serious issue, or warning people of the dangers. The group most at risk is the youth of today, because they have a high interest in sex, are good with technology, but are the least able to foresee the dangers of pornography viewing and where it will take them. They are in need of strategies to help them address their issues.

We do not necessarily have to get on a moral high horse, but I do think it is important to make a stand on some of these issues. The recovered user knows better than anyone the perils of this modern plague. If you can assist or encourage others to assist to educate upcoming generations, or to warn adult users of the dangers, then you will have done some good work.

We live in a mixed up world. Taylor and Quayle, when commenting on social trends, noted: *"Thus we create a sexualised child who we pretend to be protecting"*. If you think about this comment, especially if you turn on the TV, you will see what they mean. For example, Brats dolls are dressed in sexy clothing but are marketed to small children. While rated for mature audiences, many younger children view images from the Grand Theft Auto computer game, which has a very sexual content. A recent study by the American Psychiatric Association found that sexualised images, lyrics, fashion and role models, made girls think about and treat their own bodies as sexual objects. There is a preponderance of evidence to suggest that sexualised images and mental health outcomes for girls are a cause for concern.

Even low level sexualisation has an impact. As a society we need to talk about 'sacred intimacy'. This refers to the importance of proper sexual relationships, not just sex education. It is not just the 'how' to do it safely, but teaching about responsibility associated with being sexual. Schools in many parts of the world embrace sex education, but are fearful of making any comments about circumstances in which it is not right to do it. Moral values serve a place but, because society has moved from a religious absolute to the vocal majority, no-one is sufficiently confident to draw a line without fear of offending someone else.

When boys emerge into manhood, I think more should be done to talk about the funnel and the tunnel process and how that impacts upon their thought processes. Our children are educated and bright so we need to ensure that they have the rationale and the tools for dealing with Internet pornography problems. Boys in particular need to learn to exercise and have a life with real role models and real time relationships – not just sit in front of computers and play video games.

Men need to develop self-care skills and be more responsible for their mental wellbeing. I find it interesting that in Australia the biggest proponents for the women's movement were women. They successfully addressed many of the inequalities in the lives of women to make the world a fairer place for them. There are still areas left for women to address, but the change in last 50 years has been phenomenal. Ironically, the biggest proponent for the men's movement has been women coupled with a few exceptional men.

Nurses in country towns have actually been part of the driving force behind men's health, because they were sick of seeing the abuse men put themselves through. Being male currently means that we have a significantly shorter lifespan than women, and we are more likely to die in accidents. We men need to change the way we abuse our lives so that there is a greater equality of life with women. We can gain another 7 years if we achieve equality. Many of the psychological strategies in this book are concerned with leading a good life without various forms of self-abuse.

In summing up the need for change, a final word comes from Max Taylor and Ethel Quayle when they said that the *"public face of our society shows disapproval of the expression of sexually aggressive or demeaning acts against women and children, yet it is supportive of an industry that represents all of these things, albeit vicariously."*

Key Points

- There is a need for action to educate others, especially children, about the dangers of viewing pornography.

- As a society we need to address contradictions in sexuality – we have industries that allow children to be presented as sexualised while professing to have laws to protect children from exploitation.

- When boys emerge into manhood, more should be done to explain the funnel and the tunnel processes, and how that impacts upon their thought processes.

- Boys in particular need to learn to exercise and have a life with real role models and real time relationships – not just sit in front of computers and play video games.

Exercise 60 – Call to Action

At the risk of being a little dramatic, we are on the brink of a social crisis due to Internet pornography, online gaming and chat-lines. There is an urgent need for men and women who are willing to speak up to take action. Depending upon your role, this can be within your family, local community or society.

I have one question for you – what are you going to do? Please note some actions that you think might make a difference and put them into place, preferably sooner rather than later.

Concluding Remarks

Thank you for taking the time to work through this self-help book. I hope that you found many tools to help you on your journey of change. These tools are for you to do-it-yourself. You must learn to do it for yourself because self-control is ultimately the only control that counts.

If you have worked your way through the whole book, you have completed 60 different exercises varying from journal entries to complex psychological tasks. Underpinning it all is the need to get you off the neural highway. I hope that you have blocked some on-ramps, built new exits and off-ramps, and have an alternative route or two in the areas of your life which really matter to you. It is a complex strategy of tasks to rewire the way you approach life.

I wish that I had a compact program of researched best practice to offer a solution to you which has been tried in the research laboratory, but it has not yet been developed. I have put together as many good ideas as I could find to help you. The urgency of your problem called me to action, because I hadn't found any books which completely filled the need. It means that if you continue to have a struggle and you are not managing, keep seeking answers because psychological understanding evolves.

While I did not write this for other researchers, with a bit of luck this book will help them to develop programs in the future. However, many of the techniques discussed in this book are tried and true in other areas of psychology, and I have been piloting them in my clinical practice (so there is no reason why they will not work for you).

The key is repetition and practice. Please keep learning from your mistakes until there are no more slip-ups.

Going back to where I started, you are a man of courage to look at your problem and seek to address it. Please remember that you are more than your problem behaviour and that you can have a new future. I sincerely hope that many of the things I have shared with you in this book have changed your life and will give you the future you deserve.

In conclusion, know that all of the men I have treated, who have had success in addressing their Internet pornography problems, have new lives. They did not simply remove the pornography; they re-learnt to have fun in the real world, how to relate to real people, and how to deal with emotions in a healthy fashion. As you continue to do these things, your life will be forever changed for the better.

This has been a tremendous battle for you. It is a battle of change which is worth it for you, your family and the world around you. My dear brother, I desire for you the best of joy in your future. May your life shine brightly as you live the good life you have strived so conscientiously to achieve.

Dr Phil Watts

Useful Resources

There are quite a lot of resources available in the community, but I wrote this book because most of them do not match the needs as I perceive them to be. I have used ideas from some of these materials and I include in the following list a few of the more useful materials which incorporate ideas consistent with this book:

Patrick Carnes wrote *Out of the Shadows* (2005) and *Facing the Shadows* (2005). He also has a workbook associated with his material. You will find helpful ideas in his works as he is a sensible writer.

The *Sex Addiction Workbook* (2003) by Tamara Sbraga and William O'Donohue is a fantastic resource for sex addictions in general, with some useful ideas for Internet pornography. Some of their material was used to form my ideas, and other ideas are common to both their book and my program. I have tried to refer to their unique ideas in this book.

For those of you who fall into the more major sexual addiction-type pattern of behaviour and, in particular, if you act out the pornography problems, Canning's *Love, Anger, Lust: Understanding Sexual Addiction* (2008) is a useful introduction into this area. It is not quite as useful as a do-it-yourself treatment guide, but it is very helpful for understanding the underlying issues.

Mark Kastleman's *The Drug of the new millennium* (2007); Dennis Frederick's *Conquering Pornography* (2007); and Mark Chamberlain's *Confronting Pornography* (2005) are useful books for gaining some general background material to assist in managing the problem. These books have strong religious components, so they are particularly helpful if you have a religious background (but may be harder to read if you are from a secular background).

At the professional end, the recent book by Kimberley Young and Cristiano Nabuco de Abreu *Internet Addiction: A handbook and guide to evaluation and treatment* (2011) is a landmark work for bringing together the current research and theory for a variety of Internet addictions.

Various works by Ethel Quayle and Max Taylor in the area of child pornography have no peer. Their book *Child Pornography: an Internet crime* (2003) is an excellent resource for the professional. You will see many of these authors' ideas incorporated in this book, however, most of their books are for the treating professional, not the client.

At the professional end, the recent book by Kimberley Young and Cristiano Nabuco de Abreu Internet Addiction: A handbook and guide to evaluation and treatment (2011) is a landmark work for bringing together the current research and theory for a variety of Internet addictions. Michael Seto's book called Internet Sex Offenders (2013) is a superb reference for the professional.

There are many other professionals who, because of their work, have indirectly contributed to this book. It is exciting to be part of a rapidly growing body of knowledge.

I hope that you will find other useful materials in your journey. There are various writers in the field, as I have mentioned previously, but at this stage this is still a new frontier in which we are all trying to learn about effective treatment in this complex area.

Index

A
ABC model *see* functional behavioural assessment
abstinence 80–1, 84, 180, 212–13
acting out behaviour
   child pornography and 134, 136–7
   pornography and 45–8, 109, 112, 125, 127, 129
   triggers for 151
addiction, compulsion compared 3
addiction test 23–6
addictive behaviours 87–8
   chemicals associated with 91–8
   hormones associated with 91–8
   neurotransmitters associated with 91–8
adrenal type hormones 93
adrenalin 92, 93
advertising as pornography 67, 70–1, 177
antecedents *see* pornography use, triggers leading to
anxiety *see* mood disorders
arousal reconditioning 193–4, 198
assertiveness skills 209, 213–14
aversive conditioning 195–6, 201–2

B
behaviour, analysis of 138–42, 168–73, 216–22
behaviour chain highway 216–22
behavioural therapy 138
beliefs, analysis of 160–2
brain function
   gender differences 86–90
   impact of pornography use on 73–85

C
cartoons and caricatures as pornography 48, 50
CBT *see* cognitive behaviour therapy
chemicals, associated with addictive behaviours 91–8
child pornography 47–8, 128, 132–7
   habituation and 34, 135
   mandatory reporting requirements 132
   reasons for use of 117, 134–5
   religious users of 224–5
children, sexualisation of 242–3
classical conditioning 188
   meaning 103
cognitive behaviour therapy 96, 138, 158

Index 251

collecting behaviour 98, 107, 109, 130, 133
  child pornography and 134
  see also obsessive compulsive disorder
communication strategies 213–14, 240–1
comorbidity 95, 134
compulsion, addiction compared 3
conditioning and reinforcing aspects of pornography use 103–4, 123, 187
reconditioning techniques 90–202
consequential thinking 186, 187, 189
covert sensitisation 195, 196, 202
criminal offences *see* illegal material

D

depression *see* mood disorders
desensitisation of triggers 149–50
dopamine 92

E

educating the public about pornography problems 242–5
emotions as triggers for pornography use 112, 151–3
endorphins 92–3
epinephrine 93
extroverted personalities and pornography use 118–19

F

fantasies
  role of 192–3
  use in treatment 193–6
fetishes 68, 70, 137, 199, 201, 210
  development of 104, 105
  mandatory reporting requirements 132

focussed breathing 147–8
functional behavioural assessment 138–42
funnel *see* tunnel and funnel model

G

gender
  biological differences 76–7, 86–90
  pornography use and 61–2, 76–7
  sexual arousal and 75–6, 77, 86–90
guilt
  effects of 41–2, 48, 69, 71, 103, 105, 186, 189
  impact of religious beliefs on 11, 17, 116, 118–19, 121, 159, 224–6, 229

H

habituation 33–6, 55, 104, 119
  child pornography and 34, 135
health professionals
  ethics of 227
  mandatory reporting requirements of 130, 132
  when to seek help from 13–15, 96–8, 107, 114, 117, 134, 136, 208
help and advice
  sources of 14
  when to seek 13–15, 96–8, 107, 114, 117, 134, 136, 208
hormones, associated with addictive behaviours 91–8

I

illegal material 47–8, 68–70, 128–37
illness as trigger for pornography use 155
images, analysis of what leads to arousal 107–12
Internet addiction test 23–6

Internet pornography experience, comparison with intimate sexual experience 101–2
intimacy, re-learning 211–12
introverted personalities and pornography use 118

J
journal as self-treatment record 8

M
masturbation, use in treatment 190–201
masturbatory satiation 194–5, 200
men's health issues 243–4
mental health assessment 98
mood disorders
  identifying on timeline of life events 118
  relationship to pornography use 2, 95–8, 152–3
  relevance to recovery 91
  role of serotonin 94
  sexual dysfunction and 95
  sleeping problems 95
  treatment for 95–6
morality, impact of pornography use on 41–4, 68–70
motivational interviewing 186

N
neurotransmitters, associated with addictive behaviours 91–8
norepinephrine 93

O
objectification of women 39, 207, 215
obscene or offensive material 132
obsessive compulsive disorder 96, 98, 110
  child pornography and 134
  see also collecting behaviour
OCD see obsessive compulsive disorder
operant conditioning, meaning 103
orgasmic reconditioning 194, 199
oxytocin 93

P
physical exercise, role in mental health 169, 172
pornographic stories 47–8, 107
pornography
  accessibility of 51–6
  disposal and deletion of 130–1, 175–6, 178–9
  early exposure to 114–16
  history of 49–57
  marketing of 55, 57
  range of material encompassed by term 66–72
pornography industry 203–6
  growth of 54–5
pornography use
  characteristics of problem use 1–7, 27, 31, 59–65
  conditioning and reinforcing aspects 103–4, 123, 187
  consequences of problem use 27, 32–3, 45–8, 119, 138–9, 186–9
  impact on brain function 73–85
  impact on hormones 91–8
  impact on morality 41–4, 68–70
  impact on relationships 11, 37–40, 119, 205, 206–7, 232–41
  impact on sexual performance 39
  impact on sexuality 203–15
  legal problems 34, 45–8, 133

identification of problem use
23–36, 70, 113–22, 126
impact of technological change on
34, 50–1, 52–8, 60–1
mood disorders and 2, 95–8, 152–3
overcoming problem use 79–80
reasons for problem use 16–18,
94–5, 100–5, 108–11, 123, 133–5
user profile and characteristics 63–5
  gender 61–2, 76–7
  religion 64, 224
  sexual orientation 77
viewing behaviour 60–1, 62–3
  escalation of 124–5
see also triggers leading to pornography use
psychiatric and psychological conditions associated with uncontrolled pornography use 96
psychiatrists *see* health professionals
psychologists *see* health professionals

R

recovery
  relevance of depression and anxiety to 91
  relevance of willpower to 5–6
relapses 4–5, 81–2, 117, 140, 218–19
  analysis of 140, 141
  religious beliefs and 228
  triggers leading to 70–1
relationships
  characteristics of healthy 100–1
  impact of pornography use on 11, 37–40, 119, 205, 206–7, 232–41
  re-establishing 206, 208–9, 211–13
religion, spirituality compared 225
religious beliefs
  impact of pornography use on 11, 17, 42–3, 224–5

masturbation and 191
religious groups, pornography use among 64, 224
religious leaders, seeking help from 43, 225
religious treatment and recovery strategies 225, 228, 229, 231
risk-taking behaviour 45–8, 127–37

S

self-conditioning processes 103–4
self-control strategies 174–9, 192
sensate focus 211–12
serotonin 93–4
sexting 128
sexual arousal
  chemicals released during 91–8
  fantasies and 192–3
  gender differences 75–6, 77, 86–90
  images and 107–12
  masturbation 190–201
sexual awareness, development of 114–16
sexual dysfunction, anxiety and depression and 95
sexual experience, comparison with Internet pornography experience 101–2
sexual feelings as triggers for pornography use 151, 153–5
sexual orientation, pornography use and 77
sexual tension release 197–8
sexualisation of children 242–3
sexuality, pornography and 203–15
sleeping problems 32–3
  mood disorders and 95
  time management and 182
  as triggers for pornography use 155

social activities as replacement for pornography use 170, 172–3
software
   to control Internet usage 176
   to manage time 177
spiritual leaders, seeking help from 43
spirituality 223–31
   religion compared 225
stories *see* pornographic stories

T

technology
   impact on accessibility of pornography 51–6
   techniques to manage use of 175–9
test to identify pornography use problems 23–6
testosterone 91–2
therapists *see* health professionals
thought management techniques 158–67
time management 180–5
   role in managing behaviour 81, 171
   software 177
timeline of pornography use 113–22, 126
treatment, use of masturbation in 190–201
triggers leading to pornography use 138, 139–57
   deconditioning exercises 147–50
   desensitisation of 149–50
   external triggers 143–7
   gender differences 76
   internal triggers 143, 151–7
      emotions 112, 151–3
      illness 155
      mood disorders 152–3
      sexual feelings 151, 153–5
      sleeping problems 155
   management of 143, 147–50, 174–9
   relationship to thoughts 158–67
   restructuring of 190
   triggers leading to relapses 70–1
tunnel and funnel model 100–6, 118
   gender differences 235–6

U

urge surfing 148–9

V

values, identifying 20–2
verbal satiation 195, 201
viewing behaviour 60–1, 62–3
   escalation of 124–5

W

willpower, relevance to recovery 5–6
women, objectification of 39, 207, 215
written material *see* pornographic stories

Table of Exercises

1. Assumptions Reminder Card 7
2. Reflections Journal 8
3. Benefits and Feelings 18
4. Journal Reflections 19
5. Values 20
6. Internet Addiction Test 25
7. Porn Problem Identification 29
8. Journal Reflections 36
9. Listing the Impacts upon your Relationship 40
10. Journal Reflections 44
11. Action Time 48
12. Journal Reflections 58
13. Journal Reflections 66
14. What is Pornography? 72
15. Journal Reflections 85
16. Journal Reflections 90
17. Mental Health Assessment 98
18. Your Tunnel 105
19. Journal Reflections 106
20. Defining Your Erotica 111
21. Follow that Feeling 112
22. Timeline 121
23. Journal Activity 122
24. Timeline Variability of Use 126
25. Getting Safe 131
26. Functional Behavioural Assessment 142
27. Environmental Trigger Planning 147
28. Focussed Breathing 147
29. Urge Surfing 148
30. Desensitisation of Triggers 149
31. Journal on Sexuality 157
32. Challenging Thoughts 164
33. Thought Stopping 165
34. Escape Plan 165
35. Distraction Techniques 166
36. Journal Reflections 172
37. Becoming Physical 172
38. Finding New "Friends" 172
39. The Clean-up 179
40. Practising the Opposite 183
41. External Alarms 184
42. Time Planner 184
43. Consequential Thinking 189
44. Sexual Tension Release 197
45. Arousal Reconditioning 198
46. Orgasmic Reconditioning 199
47. Masturbatory Satiation 200
48. Verbal Satiation 201
49. Aversive Conditioning 201
50. Covert Sensitisation 202
51. Journal Reflections 210
52. Relearning Intimacy (based on Sensate Focus) 211
53. Sex Holiday 212
54. Assertiveness Skills 213
55. Making Women Real 215
56. Behaviour Chain Highway 220
57. Journal Reflections 231
58. Integrating Spiritual Tools 231
59. Talking to Your Partner 240
60. Call to Action 245

About the Author

Dr Phil Watts is a well-known Western Australian clinical and forensic psychologist and author of *Surviving the Witness Box* (2007) and *Shared Care or Divided Lives* (2008). He is an adjunct Associate Professor of Clinical Psychology at the University of Canberra.

With over 22 years' experience as a psychologist, the last 18 in private practice, he has a broad range of forensic and clinical experience. He runs a busy practice in Perth, involving forensic assessment of families and individuals and clinical treatment of adults.

A significant part of his practice is running training courses for various professions, including psychologists, social workers, lawyers and judges. Due to popular demand, he has run eleven national training circuits providing practical skills training to psychologists, including workshops on treating Internet pornography.

With over 1000 appointments as a "Single Expert" in the Family Court and 900 reports for other courts, he is highly experienced within the legal arena. He has given evidence in numerous trials in the Children's, Family, District and Supreme Courts. This has included addressing issues related to sexual crimes, risk assessment and pornography problems.

Dr Watts is also deeply religious. He strongly believes that we have a Heavenly Father who loves us and through prayer we can seek support, answers and directions to life's difficult situations. However, he is respectful towards all people and believes that everyone should have the right to follow the dictates of their own conscience.

www.ingramcontent.com/pod-product-compliance
Lightning Source LLC
Chambersburg PA
CBHW050628300426
44112CB00012B/1700